WHOLEHEARTED SUCCESS

*Top Trainers, Consultants & Speakers
Share Tips, Tools & Ideas
To Help You Enjoy Long Lasting Success!*

Compiled by Doug Smart

James &
Brookfield

J&B

Publishers

WHOLEHEARTED SUCCESS

Managing Editor: Gayle Smart
Editor: Sara Kahan
Proofreader: Laura Johnson
Book Designer: Paula Chance
Copyright ©2001

Disclaimer: This book is a compilation of ideas
from numerous experts who have each contributed a chapter.
As such, the views expressed in each chapter are those of the authors
and not necessarily the views of James & Brookfield Publishers.

For more information, contact:
James & Brookfield Publishers
P.O. Box 768024
Roswell, GA 30076
℡ 770-587-9784

Library of Congress Catalog Number 00-112264

ISBN: 0-9658893-6-X

10 9 8 7 6 5 4 3 2 1

Contents

Ignite Your Greatness: Expanding Your Self-Definition

by Snowden McFall

*"Success isn't a result of spontaneous combustion.
You must set yourself on fire."*
— Arnold Glascow

The twelve-foot strip of sizzling hot coals lit up the inky black night. Flaming orange embers and blazing sparks flew up in the frigid winter chill and hissed in the darkness. The people huddled together around the strip of fire, singing, praying, and clutching each other in their fear and elation. Some looked very peaceful, some were overjoyed, but most looked terrified. One by one, each who felt it was time stepped forward, leaving the circle of song and walking to the strip of smoldering coals.

At last it was her turn. Something inside her shifted. She felt guided by a sense of protection, alignment and purpose. Her fear magically transmuted into courage as she stepped to the edge of the coals. Her bare, pink feet emerged from the warmth of her heavy winter boots. She lifted her left foot first and gingerly placed it on the 1200° coals. "This is hot," she thought, and then she relaxed and continued the walk, feeling nothing but calm. Quickly, she checked her feet and they were not hurt, except for a tiny red spot. In that split second, she realized with amazement what she had done. She had tread on smoldering hot coals and emerged unharmed. Yes, she had a tiny sore, but most people would expect their feet to be completely burned and blistered. She had transcended the laws of nature and been lifted into a higher experience. Victorious, glowing and infinitely triumphant, she turned around and grinned broadly at her companions. "I did it!" she exclaimed, "I did it!" She was, quite simply, "Fired Up!"

That weekend was a turning point for me in 1988, as I participated in a seminar in Iowa called "Overcoming Fear and Limitation." The firewalk was the culminating exercise of a weekend filled with many wonderful lessons. I found the firewalk to be an incredible reference point that proved I could, in fact, transcend previous limitations, step forward and express the deepest part of who I am. The firewalk enabled me to confront much of my pain and confusion about my childhood. It helped me to forgive and let go of the negative self-talk and patterns ingrained inside me.

It was also an experience of expanding my self-definition. In preparing for the firewalk, Michael, the leader, who had taken thousands of people safely through firewalks, shared the nature of fear and how adrenaline affects our bodies. I learned that during a firewalk, a burst of adrenaline shifts from fear to power, allowing us to overcome traditional limitations. There are tribes in Africa who roll their entire bodies through fire to rid themselves of disease. And many of us have read stories about mothers who miraculously lift cars off their children. All of this showed me the power of the heart, coupled with purpose and God's help. It demonstrated the phenomenal value of being "Fired Up!", wherein your greatness is ignited and you can succeed in ways you never thought possible.

Against All Odds

Have there ever been times in your life when you did something you thought you couldn't do? When you exceeded your own expectations and were truly wonderful in the moment? For some of you, it was a sporting event, where you broke all the local teams' records or got that home run. One of my friends swears that the day she jumped out of a plane skydiving forever changed her life. For others, it might be a time at work when you were called upon to do an extraordinary task within a ridiculous amount of time and you did it. You pulled it off! Against all odds, you succeeded! Those moments of greatness, just like mine in the firewalk, are pivotal in our lives, for they are the times when we expand beyond our self-definition and "break out of the box" of how we traditionally perceive ourselves. Those transcendent moments can forecast success in so many areas of your life. They can mean the difference between a mediocre existence or one in which your very essence radiates to the world as a shining example of someone living his or her dreams.

The Magic Ingredient for Greatness: Defining Yourself as a Winner

What makes some succeed and others fail? Why did Marion Jones have a clear vision of winning five gold medals in the 2000 Olympics and go on to win three golds and two bronzes when others paled by comparison? Although all who participated were exceptional athletes, there had to be a completely different mindset in Marion's consciousness. Marion Jones was going to win — no matter what. It was not a statement of arrogance or prowess. It was more a clear affirmation which she confidently projected in every event. Her box of self-definition portrayed her as a winner — victorious in all the track events she competed in. Her box was big and victorious. Is yours? If you're like most people, it probably isn't as big as it could be, largely because of the way you were raised.

Lessons from Childhood

From the time we are little children, our boxes of self-definition begin forming. How many of you had parents who told you that you could do anything, that you were a terrific human being, that you were destined for greatness? If you did, congratulations. You must have a very large box. Unfortunately, that is not the experience most of us had. Part of it had to do with our exploration of the world and what happened when we tried new things. A national research study on toddlers demonstrated that 75 percent of the feedback most little ones received was negative: "Don't do that!" "Stop!" " Watch out!" That's what we were told most of the time.

It's not because our parents were inherently bad; it's because toddlers get into everything, which you know if you have raised one. Our parents were trying to keep us safe. But often in doing so, the negative programming imprinted our psyche, and our self-definition box began to have limits. We learned that there are many things we couldn't do. And we believed that — even if it wasn't true.

So, as we grew up and experienced new challenges, we internalized that inner critic, who judged us when we didn't do things perfectly the first time. And who does? Very few professional athletes were magnificent in their chosen sport the day they first tried it. You've probably heard the story of how Michael Jordan was cut from his high school basketball team. How did he get to his level of greatness? By tenacity and practice, vision and determination, by creating a new box for himself. One thousand shots a day — that's how many he used to take when he practiced for professional basketball. He expanded his self-definition and saw himself as masterful. He changed his inner perception and made his box bigger than it had been when he was in high school.

What About You: How Big is Your Box?

A very simple way to answer this question is to look at your life. Take a moment to fill out this chart and do the math at the end. You may be surprised at the outcome.

Exercise 1- How Big is Your Box Right Now?

Yes ☐ No ☐ 1. Are you generally happy with your life?

Yes ☐ No ☐ 2. Are you doing work that you truly enjoy?

Yes ☐ No ☐ 3. Are you earning a good salary for your efforts?

Yes ☐ No ☐ 4. Are you challenged and excited by your work?

Yes ☐ No ☐ 5. Do you feel valued and appreciated for your insights and intelligence?

Yes ☐ No ☐ 6. Are you stretching and growing on a regular basis?

Yes ☐ No ☐ 7. Are you excited to get up and start your day?

Yes ☐ No ☐ 8. Is your personal life fulfilling and meaningful?

Yes ☐ No ☐ 9. Do you have people in your life who love you?

Yes ☐ No ☐ 10. Do you often spend time laughing with friends?

Yes ☐ No ☐ 11. Do you have moments of peace and quiet in every day?

Yes ☐ No ☐ 12. Is your health good?

Yes ☐ No ☐ 13. Do you take care of yourself?

Yes ☐ No ☐ 14. Do you go on vacation at least twice a year?

Yes ☐ No ☐ 15. Do you have any kind of spiritual faith or religious practice?

Yes ☐ No ☐ 16. Are you living the life of your dreams?

Yes ☐ No ☐ 17. Do you feel blessed in your life?

Yes ☐ No ☐   18. Are you settling for a "safe" position?

Yes ☐ No ☐   19. Are you afraid to rock the boat for fear of reprisal?

Yes ☐ No ☐   20. Are you in a dead-end position that offers very
                   little stimulation?

Yes ☐ No ☐   21. Would you rather roll over and stay in bed than
                   go to work?

Yes ☐ No ☐   22. Do you worry frequently?

Yes ☐ No ☐   23. Are you overcommitted financially?

Yes ☐ No ☐   24. Do you feel like you'll never get out from under?

Yes ☐ No ☐   25. Do you have lots of frustrations in your life?

Yes ☐ No ☐   26. Do you feel like there's no time in the day for you?

Yes ☐ No ☐   27. Do you overcommit to others?

Yes ☐ No ☐   28. Do you feel cursed with bad luck?

Yes ☐ No ☐   29. Is life passing you by?

Yes ☐ No ☐   30. Is there anything you always have wanted
                   to do but haven't?

Rating: Give yourself one point for every *yes* answer to questions 1-17. Give yourself one point for every *no* answer to questions 18-30.

Scoring: 25-30 Your life is terrific — your box of self-definition is very big and you live in an expansive state. Congratulations!

Scoring: 20-24 You are doing very well with your life and your box is growing and healthy. You know how to expand and how to succeed. Keep applying those techniques in all areas of your life and you'll be richly rewarded. Great work!

Scoring: 16-19 You're more than halfway there to living the life of your dreams. Some things are going very well in your life, and yet there is big room for improvement in others. Watch out for self-limitations.

Start putting your focus on winning in the problem areas and you'll be amazed what happens.

Scoring: 11-15 Your box is quite limited. You have had some moments of joy and success, but for whatever reason, you are holding yourself back. You can have more and be happier. It's time to start thinking about yourself. It's time to start winning more often.

Scoring: 1-10 Your box is almost tiny. You've had a tough time and your life is not what you want it to be. There is so much more you could have in your life and you don't yet believe that. It's time for you to reframe and reexamine your priorities and start living life more on your terms. You deserve more joy and happiness. You can have it — but it's going to require a shift in your self-definition. You are worthy of more.

How did you do? Are you where you want to be? Most of us have some work to do. There are some tips in the pages ahead that will help you expand your box in larger and better ways and help you to have more joy and success in the coming years. And don't think that I have all the answers. I just have some clues.

My Box Was Tiny

When I look back at my life, I see how far I have come and how far I still have to go. In my early twenties, I was a very unhappy young lady, with little confidence in myself on any level. Having grown up in an alcoholic family with a terminally ill mother, I became super-responsible at a very young age and was good at taking care of everyone except myself.

I had attracted the wrong kind of man, who convinced me that I was unintelligent, unattractive and that no one else would want me. Even though I had a B.A. from Vassar College with honors and a Masters Degree from Brown University, I listened to him. Male teachers at the school where I worked told me I was attractive, even pretty, but I didn't believe them. My self-esteem was just too low.

Fortunately, I realized that something was not right. I began therapy and started working on myself. I learned all about ACOA (Adult Children of Alcoholics) behaviors and how to start taking better care of myself. I enrolled in several personal development courses and learned to recognize my own worth. It took years and years of new programming, new lessons, and new experiences for me to expand my tiny box of self-definition into something bigger and better, something truer to who I really am.

Today, I am deeply grateful for my life. As the owner of a of successful advertising and training company I founded in 1983, I have learned how to balance my life and take care of myself. I have been honored at the White House for my non-profit work helping female entrepreneurs succeed and appeared on CNN and Bloomberg Television. After decades of dating the wrong men, God blessed me with a fabulous husband 11 years ago, and we recently renewed our vows and went on a second honeymoon. This is the fourth book I have authored/co-authored, and I am working on two more manuscripts. My spiritual development is very important to me, and I now have a lovely family of choice — dear friends that I love and that love me and we enjoy and encourage each other.

There are still many areas for improvement and many challenges for me to overcome. I need to do a better job on exercise and fitness, and keeping my stress levels balanced. I still make plenty of mistakes and each day is a learning opportunity. But I know that my box of self-definition has drastically changed when I see what has happened over the last 20 years. The same thing can happen for you.

How Do You Expand Your Box?

Ok — you've taken the test and you have some work to do. How do you get your box to be bigger than it is today? It can actually be easier than you might think.

1. Start with Your Daily Successes

In a course called *Technologies for Creating,* the instructor told us to record ten successes each day for a week. Initially, we all reacted with groans and wondered how we could ever find ten things to record. But as I got in the habit, I began to notice that my consciousness was changing. Successes were not huge events, but rather daily actions that I took and accomplished. I actually continued with this activity for close to a year, and it is amazing what happened. At the end of the year, I had a full book of successes and as I looked it over, I realized that I was an effective person, that I got things done. This realization started to stretch my box and I started viewing myself differently. The same thing will be true for you — try it. You might start your list with "Got out of bed," because there are days when you don't want to do that.

2. Share the Good News

We live in a negative society which focuses on negative news. Every workplace has an 'ain't it awful' club in the lunchroom, gossiping about all the bad news and stirring up trouble. Avoid this group religiously and start asking your co-workers: "What's the good news?" By focusing on the positive, you'll have to find good news in your day, too, that will start the box expanding, as you develop more gratitude for the good things in your life.

3. Do a Personal Inventory

Find some quiet time when you won't be disturbed, and be really honest with yourself. Make a list of your "I Can's." These are the things that you do very well, no matter how seemingly small or insignificant to you. Once you read it over, you'll realize that there are many talents and gifts you have that you probably have not given yourself credit for. It's time you started to appreciate your abilities and recognize your own greatness.

4. Ask for Positive Feedback from People Who Believe in You and Listen to It

This one may be a little uncomfortable if you're not used to receiving compliments. If your box is small, it may be a new experience to hear someone else say good things about you. But do this anyway. Ask someone you know who loves or respects you to give you some honest, positive feedback about how they view you and what they think makes you great. Ask them to give you only positive feedback and tell you what your gifts and strengths are and why they believe in you. If you're really determined to stretch your box, tape-record their comments. And offer to do the same thing for them. You'll be delighted and perhaps pleasantly surprised by what you hear. I can guarantee that your box will start growing if you truly take this exercise to heart.

5. Accept an Invitation to Do Something You Never Considered

Often, others perceive us much more positively than we view ourselves. It's been said that we are frequently our own harshest critic, and that certainly is true of me. Sometimes others see your gifts so clearly that they invite you to events or leadership roles that you would never have sought on your own. Accept these invitations and see what happens. You might just end up stepping into your own greatness.

Walking Among the Great

I had an experience with this a few years ago. Much to my surprise, I received an invitation to an event that forever changed my life, and parts of me were so surprised that I had been asked to go. The invitation read, "The Dunfey Family and Directors of Global Citizens Circle warmly invite you to participate in our first 'Southern Circle' Sunday, January 17, 1999, in collaboration with the 14th Annual Martin Luther King Jr. commemoration weekend." Also attending were Nobel Peace Prize recipients: John Hume from Northern Ireland, Archbishop Desmond Tutu from South Africa, Coretta Scott King, and Ambassador Andrew

Young. When I received this card in the mail, I was stunned. And thrilled. And wondered how I had been invited.

But this transplanted Southerner who had grown up amid the strife and unrest of the Civil Rights Movement in the 1960's, responded with a resounding "Yes!" and I went to Atlanta and had one of the most unforgettable experiences of my life.

What moved me was not the impressive nature of these human beings, although their accomplishments were considerable and world-renowned. What really moved me about each of these people was their humanity. As I sat with Leah Tutu, the Archbishop's wife, I was struck by her generosity of spirit and incredible courage. When she took the stage to receive an award for her humanitarian work, she coyly turned to her husband and said "Darling, how does it feel to have ME be the one getting the award?" We all laughed and he was thrilled for her. John Hume, who normally appears on the news as a very serious and stern leader, is actually delightful and friendly. Just like I would be, he was nervous about his speech and pleased that he had done well. He embraced his family warmly afterwards and introduced them around. But the individual who most dazzled me was Archbishop Desmond Tutu. While describing atrocities that you and I can never begin to imagine in our worst nightmares, he did so with such love and forgiveness in his eyes and voice. I knew that I was unquestionably in the presence of greatness, and it touched me forever.

It also helped me break out of the box of self-definition about my ability to impact others on a large scale because I saw that it was their very essence, their passion and commitment which made these people great.

6. Network with People More Successful Than You

As a professional speaker, I am blessed to know other speakers who have inspired millions with their wit and wisdom. I once heard Mark Victor Hansen tell a story about Tony Robbins. He and Tony were both presenting in front of a huge stadium of people. Later, off stage, Mark asked Tony why Tony was so much more prosperous when Mark was doing many of the same things. Tony said that he had billionaires in his Master Mind Group and that he learned from them. Mark realized he wasn't associating with others at that level of success and he changed his habits. Today, he is a multi-millionaire, and you know him best as the co-author of the hugely successful book series, *Chicken Soup for the Soul*. His friend and co-author, Jack Canfield, has also come to enjoy a very affluent lifestyle, all because he expanded his box. Twenty years ago, Jack had trouble asking for $600 as a speaking fee in the education market. Today he easily commands $25,000+ a speech and he is booked for years. That's a major expansion of his box.

You can do the same thing. Start associating with those more successful than you. Offer to buy an industry leader lunch and sit back and listen. Ask questions, take notes, learn, contribute. Write a thank you note and stay in touch. Rub elbows with others you consider to be great and give back. The more successful the people you associate with, the more successful you will be, in every area of your life.

7. Join a Master Mind Group

There are many good sources on the market for this. The most effective ones seem to be comprised of professionals who are all working on plans for the future and willing to support and encourage each other. They meet weekly and track their progress and they invite information and feedback. I joined one myself a year ago, and I can tell you that it has made a substantial difference in my life. Part of it is the focus and part of it is having to be accountable to others about your goals and accomplishments.

8. Reference Your Moments of Greatness

One of the best ways to recognize your own greatness is to review what you have already accomplished in your life.

Expanding Your Self-Definition

Experiences	*New Self-Definitions*
1. Did 10K road race.	*Learned I could overcome pain and be strong; that I have stamina!*
2. Raised $3,000 for cancer.	*Learned to ask others for help for good cause and share about my brother's illness.*
3. Started at-home business.	*Learned I can take risks and be an entrepreneur.*
4. Became top distributor for first quarter in my region.	*Saw I can share my enthusiasm for my products and get others excited, too.*
5. Put on one-day seminar for my group.	*Learned I am a good organizer and networker. Others like my style and want to work with me.*

Expanding Your Box Activity

Take ten minutes now and do this activity. Get yourself a pen or pencil and a piece of paper.

Step 1. Make two columns. On the left side, label the column "Experiences." Make a list of any extraordinary experiences you have had in your life, any time when your self-definition changed. These need not be new record setters, simply experiences which were new and exciting for you. All that matters is that they changed your self-perception. Give yourself credit for all you have accomplished in your life and observe how you have expanded your self-definition.

Review every area of your life: physical, personal, professional, academic, spiritual, arts-related, mental, psychological, romantic, financial. Have you had any notable athletic accomplishments? Have you started a business from scratch? Have you met what seemed like an impossible goal or deadline? How have you overcome your fear and triumphed? Have you ever tried skydiving or parasailing? Write it down. Give yourself credit for what you have already done.

Step 2. Now that you have your list, take a few minutes to read it over. On the right side of the page, head the column with the word "New Self-Definitions." Next to each experience, write the expanded self-perception that you gained from that experience. See the chart here for an example.

Nothing listed here is a superhuman feat, and yet they are all important accomplishments. When you expand your self-definition, you can move on to even greater things.

9. Learn from Your Mistakes

The individuals who truly exemplify greatness to me are those who are vulnerable and honest and who keep getting up after they fall. There are no perfect human beings out there. We all make mistakes. It's just a matter of what you do about it. Instead of beating yourself up over every misstep, stop and study the situation.

What did you learn from the experience, how can you grow from it, how can you expand from it so you don't make the same mistake again? Recently, I had a a car accident which taught me some lessons in new ways.

The Crash

I had never seen so much blood. Dark red blood everywhere, seeping out of the poor young man who had just crashed into my car with his speeding motorcycle. In a split second, both of our lives changed forever. He spent weeks in the hospital with broken bones and

100 stitches. Other than a mangled car, my wounds were hidden on the inside. That afternoon came and went with sickening finality. And as I put him on prayer lists of different organizations and checked on his condition, I wondered what the various lessons were for me.

Now, nearly two months later, I have begun to make sense of this. Thankfully, he is on his way to full recovery and will be fine. My mangled car has been traded in for something that didn't have so many memories attached. The most important work was forgiveness of myself. Although the police at the scene did not find me at fault, I felt terribly guilty for having been in an accident in which another human being was hurt. I'm still working on letting that go, to surrender it all to God and to realize that events happen in our lives that allow us to learn and grow. But I know there were many miracles that day. Even though my car had $5,600 worth of damage and the driver's side, steering column, and dash board were crushed, I was unharmed. There had to be an angel there protecting me. The young man did not have a helmet on and yet did not suffer severe head wounds or a concussion. Again, another angel looking out for him. There was a witness who saw me stop at the stop sign and testified for the police. There were people on the scene within seconds of the accident. There was so much grace that day that I now can reference the event as miraculous — a time when two people who could have been killed were very lucky. And I now approach my car and driving from a whole new perspective, one filled with gratitude and awe. Instead of judging myself harshly for the whole experience, I learned something new and different about my life. Every experience you have is an opportunity for growth. It may take awhile to see it, but the opportunity is there for you.

10. Look to Sources of Inspiration

One of the best ways to expand your box is to listen to those who inspire you. Whether it's your grandmother who has wonderful pearls of wisdom or your favorite preacher or motivational speaker, there are others out there who have great wisdom to share. These people can often help you look at your life from a new perspective and give you the chance to see yourself differently. Whatever fires you up, do it! Listen to uplifting music, watch winners succeed, read inspirational stories. Do whatever it takes to start looking at your life from a more expansive place.

Your Greatness Lies Within

Throughout this chapter, I have deliberately not defined greatness for you, because I believe each person's definition is unique. I do think that greatness is far simpler than most people make it, that it is an intrinsic quality that each individual possesses which can be expressed in a myriad of ways, from tiny acts of kindness to monumental acts of world peace. The levels of greatness inside each person are limitless. It's only a matter of accessing that part of ourselves and nurturing it, sharing it and expressing it. You have all the gifts inside you that you will ever need. Take the time to expand your box, do these techniques and see what happens. The world will be a poorer place if you don't share your gifts. Expand your box today and ignite your greatness. It takes only one match to start a roaring fire!

ABOUT SNOWDEN MCFALL

Snowden is a dynamic professional speaker, author and trainer. The author of two books, Fired Up! How to Succeed By Making Your Dreams Come True *and* Let's Get Fired Up!*, and co-author of* Exceptional Accomplishment, *she is also President and owner of Brightwork Advertising and Training, a full service business she founded in 1983. As an expert in business success strategies, her presentations focus on motivation, marketing, time management, project management, customer retention, presentation skills and overcoming and preventing burnout.*

An active community citizen, Snowden was named the National Woman in Business Advocate of the Year by the Small Business Administration for her work in helping female entrepreneurs. This led to a White House ceremony and a congressional luncheon in her honor. Snowden was also chosen as finalist for Inc. Magazine*'s New England Entrepreneur of the Year Award. A graduate of Vassar College with a Master's Degree from Brown University, Snowden is an active member of the National Speakers Association. Founder of International Fired Up! Month in October, she has appeared on over 300 radio stations nationwide. She was recently featured on CNN and Bloomberg Television and has appeared in* Entrepreneurial Woman, Inc. Magazine *and* Adweek *as well as the* World's Who's Who of Women, *and* Who's Who in Emerging Leaders in America.

Contact Information:
Snowden McFall
Fired Up!
74 Northeastern Blvd., #20
Nashua, NH 03062
Phone: (603) 882-0600
Fax: (603) 882-5979
E-mail: SMcFall@FiredUp-TakeAction-Now.com
Websites: www.FiredUp-TakeAction-Now.com
www.BrightworkAdvertising.com

LIVING AN AUTHENTIC LIFE

by Max Howard

T he theater is the most competitive, brutal, emotionally wrenching, financially insecure business in the world. In any given year, of the 38,000 members of Actors Equity Association, the professional union of stage actors in America, 55 percent of the membership will be unemployed. Of the remaining 45 percent who do find employment, it will be for an annual average income of less than $6,300. When you stop to consider that a Broadway star can make from $20,000 to $50,000 a week, it is obvious that for most of the few who do find work, it is for cab fare and coffee. Why do we do it?

Because we must. Because our integrity, responsibility and passion require it of us. And so it should be for us all. The behavior of every man, woman and child on earth should be based on integrity, responsibility and passion.

But what does an actor know about authenticity? Aren't actors fakes? Frauds? Fictions? We put on costumes and makeup, change the way we walk and talk, even how we think and feel, all in the name of make-believe. How can actors know anything about authenticity?

Because what you, the audience, see is secondary to what you feel. And what you feel is what the actor feels, his connection with his deepest, most human, most personal self, speaking through the character he plays. What we share, the audience and the actor, is our common life experience, our humanity, our essential selves. Actors are most successful when they are most authentic. And by definition, to be authentic is to be "entitled to acceptance or belief." Ultimately, beyond talent, looks, charm, voice and grace, all the actor really has to offer is himself, his authentic self, his very presence.

Living an authentic life is enormously challenging. Integrity, responsibility and passion do not allow for excuses. But living an authentic life is also enormously rewarding! Imagine the authentic salesman whose very presence inspires confidence and trust in customers and clients. Imagine the authentic leader whose very presence inspires certainty and belief. Imagine the authentic communicator whose presence alone inspires credibility and conviction.

There is no mystery here. Living an authentic life does not require esoteric knowledge or great spiritual gifts. It does require commitment and choice. If you choose to live life everyday reaffirmed in your worth and renewed in your purpose, then commit yourself everyday to maximizing your presence on the earth.

- Know who you are.
- Know what you want. Really.
- Live fearlessly.
- Serve something greater than yourself.
- Never quit.

Know Who You Are

Self-awareness is the foundation upon which the actor builds his technique. If you don't know who you are, how can you possibly know others? This is the beginning of human understanding. Actors learn very early that all human beings, fictional or real, are either like us or unlike us. If that sounds simplistic, remember that none of us has any other point of reference but our own experience. We only know what we know. We may be empathetic, sympathetic, insightful, clever and wise, but the only life experience we have is of our own lives. Therefore, the better, the more deeply and unflinchingly we know and accept ourselves, the more able we are to comprehend and appreciate other people, their values, desires, strengths and weaknesses. How do we feel and *how do we react* when we are angry, afraid, calm, happy, jealous, envious, nervous, embarrassed, frustrated, gentle and jolly? Why do we react to certain people and specific situations the way we do? What makes us impatient and what makes us passionate? Achieving this level of self-awareness, becoming sensitive to the full experience of being alive at all, is what connects us to authors, audiences, characters and history. It will connect you, too. This is the very heart of leadership.

There are also issues of integrity here. Who are you when nobody's looking? Who are you when you're all alone? What are you thinking when you're talking (what actors call subtext)? What choices do you make when the consequences of your choices will be known by others and when they will be known only to you? Do you always follow the rules or do you bend them and break them according to your own sense of right and wrong? And are you understanding and forgiving of others who might make those same choices for themselves?

One of my favorite stories is of the craftsmen and masons who built the great cathedrals of Europe in the Middle Ages. At the top of the vaults, on the cornices, on the capitals of the columns, so high above the floor that no one can see it, the detail work is as complete and fine as it is on the altars and the windows at floor level. These men were asked why they took such pains and care to do such fine work when it wouldn't be seen. "Oh," they said, "But it will be seen! God will see it!" From time to time it's good to ask ourselves how the work is going at the top of our own cathedrals.

As we do our work, staying focused on who we are, how we think and feel and what our motives are can be difficult and tedious. Such focus requires devotion, motivation and excellent tools. Interestingly, one of the most powerful and reliable self-awareness tools is pain, whether physical, emotional, psychological or spiritual. When we are in pain, whether from boredom, fear, stress or anger, we are in a state of heightened human consciousness which brings a state of heightened human awareness and that almost always provides an optimum learning opportunity. Humans try to avoid pain and quite rightly so, but we will experience pain all the same because it's part of being alive. So rather than regarding pain as your enemy, something to be ignored, avoided or denied, accept pain as your ally. Pain not only tells us that something is wrong, it tells us where. Its intensity tells us how acute our problem is.

Self-awareness skills continue to develop as we mature and grow in experience, like putting an ever-finer edge on a cutting blade. They are powerful skills to have, in business and in life, helping you connect ever more quickly and deeply with everyone you meet, giving insight and understanding into their motives, their experiences and the realities of their lives. It might be said that self-awareness is our most reliable human connection.

Exercise: Next Monday morning, as you begin your drive to work, put a tape recorder in the seat beside you and turn it on. Forget that it's there. When you get to work, turn it off. On your return trip home that evening, turn the recorder on again and when you arrive home shut it off. Do this all week. On the weekend, find a quiet time, take your recorder, rewind, hit play and listen to yourself. You might learn something that surprises you.

Know What You Want . . . Really

"I never want to work again!" Why? "Because I hate my job." Why? "Because it's stupid." Why? "Because it's boring and there's nothing creative about it." Why? "Because my boss just wants me to do what I'm told, when I'm told, the way I'm told to do it." Why? "Because he's afraid I'll do something that will show him up!" Does this person "never want to work again" or does this person want to do meaningful work and be recognized for it?

"I want to be rich!" Why? "So I can have everything I want." Why? "So I never have to worry about paying the bills again." Why? "Because I'm tired of being afraid all the time." Does this person want to be rich or does this person want to be free of fear? And will money make him fearless?

At a time of great turmoil in my life, when I didn't know which way to turn, what to do, which path to take, I came across an old exercise. The author said, in so many words, don't just do the exercise, take it seriously. This was the exercise: it's the day of your funeral and you are there. What do you want to see and what do you want to hear?

I was astonished by the vision that came to me! I wanted my two children to stand and say, "He loved us and we knew it. We loved him and he knew it." That was all. Everything else could be as it was, but I wanted to see and hear that. In that moment, my life changed. From the time I was eight years old I had been focused on a single goal: to be a performer, an entertainer and an actor in the theater. Now, for the first time in my life, it didn't matter to me if I were an actor or if I were rich or famous or just another guy. What I wanted was what my vision had brought me.

I met my son and daughter when they were thirteen and eleven respectively. As parent-to-children, we had our challenges. I can truthfully say that our family has earned itself, for we have had to decide, to choose, what we would be or if we would be at all. It had to start with me, of course, because I was the adult and it was up to me to love them first, unconditionally and to love them always, regardless of how they might finally feel about me. But my children, now adults, are fair, caring people and learned for themselves very quickly that the best way to receive unconditional love is to give it. That is why we don't think in terms of "stepfather" or "stepchildren" in our family. I am their father and they are my children.

Being able to visualize yourself in a variety of life circumstances is an important tool for learning what you want and another reason to have well-developed self-awareness skills. When I was eighteen and ready to go to college, I knew I had to choose what I wanted to do for the rest of my life. I chose the theater, first because I loved it so much and because, in spite of the warnings I received from teachers and parents about the risk and rejection, the struggle and pain, I understood what it must be like to live a life of regret. I didn't want to be at the end of my life and look back and say, "I wish I'd tried! What might have been if only I had tried?" The sadness of such an end would have been unbearable. Better the risk than the regret.

Knowing what you want, really, is only half of the equation, of course. There is also the matter of taking responsibility for your choice. From childhood we are told, "Be careful what you wish for because you just might get it." That is wise to remember, for no choice comes without challenge, without the unexpected. We make choices when we are young and then life changes, society changes, our body, hearts and minds change and the world in which we made our first choice is gone. There are always consequences, always complications. Take full responsibility for every aspect of your life. Make no one else responsible for who you are and who you become. This gives you control. Power over you does not rest outside yourself. Otherwise, you will forever be dependent upon and disappointed by other people.

For those in business, knowing what you want sustains two very important business practices: creating shared visions and setting priorities. Dreams are reached when you climb the stair steps of goals. Both are built by knowing what you want, really.

Exercise: It's the day of your funeral and you're there. What do you want to see and what do you want to hear? (Don't just do this exercise. Take it seriously. It might change your life.)

Live Fearlessly!

The greatest antidote to fear is personal passion. Fear can paralyze you, locking you in harm's way. That is why at the beginning of World War II President Franklin Roosevelt counseled the citizens of the United States that "we have nothing to fear but fear itself." By definition, passion is "any emotion of compelling force" and to compel is "to force or drive, especially to a course of action." In the army, the combat soldier is taught that in moments of crisis, do something. Anything! Take action! Even if it's wrong, do something! Why? Because only through action can the situation be resolved. And even in a crisis when you are unprepared or don't know what you're doing, you can take correct action, even by accident. Not taking action guarantees failure or death. When I began my career as a professional magician, I did so by performing in the streets of New York City, working the crowd and passing my hat. At the time I was living in Brooklyn, an actor "at liberty," and I needed a job. In New York, if you want to perform, you are welcome in the streets. There you will find classical string quartets, bluegrass bands, rock n' roll singers, magicians, jugglers, comics, poets and madmen. Everybody's welcome! You need only the courage to try.

I had been working in the streets for only a short while, really struggling, just learning the trade and not doing very well. I was inexperienced, the weather had been bad and the crowds were thin. The rent was due and I didn't have the money. The pressure was on, stress was high, anxiety was growing. One day, as I started for the train to Manhattan to work the streets, I suddenly felt the tell-tale signs in my back that told me I was about to have a major muscle spasm. For years

I had been plagued with back spasms that came periodically (usually associated with tension and stress) and left me, literally, unable to walk, for days at a time.

I lay down on the floor of my apartment, on my side, and began to breathe deeply, saying over and over, "Relax, relax, relax, relax . . ." Slowly the muscles did begin to relax and my panic began to fade. In time, I got to my feet, walked to the train and went to the streets. The story has a happy ending: it was a good weekend and the financial crisis passed. Now when I recall that day, I remember it as the day I was literally frozen with fear, the day I learned how fear itself can be a greater threat than the crisis that provokes it.

Each time we face fear we grow in courage. And courage is a state of being. Slowly, then, like acquiring gold, we acquire courage (and confidence) and when the crisis comes, we are ready. Courage is not the absence of fear but taking action in spite of our fear. And fear, like pain, is our friend. It tells us that something is seriously wrong, that we are in danger. It is another "optimum learning opportunity" that lets us grow in self-knowledge. In our daily lives, how often do we have fearful thoughts, thoughts of loss, lack, need and want? When we say, "I can't; they'll never choose me; I'm not good enough; they'll find out I'm a fake; I could never do that; I don't want to try, I'll make a fool of myself; I don't deserve it," we are expressing our fear.

The ancient philosophers believed that there are only two emotions: love and fear. And fear is the absence of love.

Exercise: Put a rubber band around your wrist and every time you think or say a negative thought, snap the rubber band against your wrist hard! Every time you say "I can't," *snap out of it!* Every time you think "I'm not good enough," or express a thought of loss or lack, *snap out of it!* This will help you change the way you think and what you feel. It will help you grow in self-awareness.

Serve Something Greater Than Yourself

I have always believed that if businesses operated as well as first-class theater companies, productivity would quadruple, problems would be halved and profits would soar! Why? The men and women who compose a theatrical ensemble are among the most intelligent, sensitive, egocentric, emotional, opinionated, obsessive, highly trained and passionate human beings one could imagine. And yet, at eight o'clock every night, in a stunning display of great teamwork, they come together to create something powerful and unique: the performance of a great play.

There may be thirty to forty craftsmen, technicians, designers, writers, composers, musicians, directors and actors who compose the company. They will be from as widely divergent socioeconomic, ethnic and educational backgrounds as you could imagine, with political and philosophical opinions ranging from the conservative to the liberal. And yet they work together with a precision, dedication and intimacy that is breathtaking. How is it possible? Because they are there to serve something greater than themselves! They serve the play, the author, the audience and, most of all, the theater itself. In a craft thousands of years old, each of them finds their own place to serve the idea, the art, the reality that is the theater and their passion.

It is incredibly liberating! To experience such skill, intelligence, dedication and effort focused on a single thought, moment to moment, in the high-risk environment of the live stage play is astonishing. Consider also that the work of the ensemble is publicly criticized by press and patrons, that everyone involved is effectively unemployed (every show is a limited run) and that the nature of the business is so uncertain that for most people the working conditions alone prove too distracting to focus effectively on the task at hand. Now you have an even more amazing display of what can happen when human beings are devoted, committed and daring enough to put something else before themselves and their own personal concerns.

What do you suppose is the intrinsic value of a Picasso painting? Two hundred dollars, perhaps, for canvas, wood and paint? And yet a Picasso will sell for five million and more any day it becomes available. Why? Certainly there are market factors and vanity factors and greed factors. But fundamentally, the Picasso, like any fine work of art that touches and inspires the viewer, is *greater than the sum of its parts*. That is the essence of art. When that is achieved, something splendid and transcending has been created. Something so splendid, in fact, that accomplished men and women, some with the education and training to rival that of a brain surgeon's, will labor long, hard and well under the most trying circumstances just for the sheer joy of participating. Imagine what your business could be if that opportunity were available to everyone in your company.

Passion, of course, is a major part of this equation. For one of the great truths about living in passion is this: Passion always begins as service and becomes leadership. We start with an overwhelming desire to serve, to be near, to learn as much as we can about that for which we feel so powerfully and in time, having acquired knowledge, experience and expertise, we begin to lead and teach and show others how to make their dreams come true. In life and in business, in politics and in sports, in every human endeavor, we will always succeed when we devote ourselves to helping others succeed first.

Exercise: Volunteer. Become a part of something that attracts you for what you can give and not for what you can take. One of my most valuable life experiences was volunteering for the American Red Cross to entertain children in the burn unit of a county hospital. What an awesome display of courage and forbearance these children presented! Uncomplaining, attentive, appreciative.

One mother said to me, "Thank you for coming. My son was

smiling when you left. It's only the second time he's smiled in the year since he was burned." How much more could one ever hope to be paid?

Never Quit

Of all the life skills required to find and live an authentic life, this is my favorite! Persistence is an act of faith. It does not require training, special skills, talent or even intelligence. It requires will: the determination to put one foot in front of the other over and over again until the journey is over.

When I was in elementary school and first participated in school athletics as a member of the basketball team, I realized at once that I was going to be a long-distance runner, that persistence was my greatest asset. Other boys were bigger, faster, stronger, more athletic, better coordinated, more determined and much more aggressive. But I would not quit. I was steady, careful, attentive and persistent. I was there, learning and working at it, every day. That's persistence. It paid off, too, when our star center, Benny Shortridge, was injured in a game against a very good team from a very tough school and I had to take his place. For the first time since joining the team, I scored points, made rebounds and played good defense. We won. After the game our coach, Mr. Thompson, told me how proud of me he was and how happy he was for me. It was the first time he told me what he thought coaching boys was all about. He said, "Mr. Howard, I've always felt like this: give me a boy with 90 percent aptitude and 10 percent attitude and I can't do a thing with him; give me a boy with 90 percent attitude and 10 percent aptitude and I'll make him a basketball player!" I swelled with pride! I didn't mind that my aptitude was so low because I had other plans for my attitude!

Never quit. Persistence is the most important skill you need to make your dreams come true.

***Exercise*:** Create or break a habit. Give yourself a period of time, your choice. It can be a day, a week, a month. Change your behavior in some way. Stop smoking. Quit drinking. Give up caffeine. Stop desserts. Write your mother regularly. Do a chore consistently. Create or break a habit. Make it something meaningful and make the time reasonable. Stick with it by the day, the hour and the minute. Be aware of what it takes and how challenged you feel. And remember that all you have to do is be persistent. You can make a new habit or change an old one in thirty days. Go for it!

There is a wonderful story told about an order of monks who lived in a monastery in Europe about 100 years ago. They were relaxing in their community room one evening after their day of prayer and labor, some talking, some reading and a few playing billiards, one of their favorite pastimes. Eventually the conversation turned to this: What would you do if the Messiah came back to earth tonight, right now?

Many of the monks said they would go straight away to the chapel and pray fervently to be forgiven their sins. Others said they would go to the fields and kiss the earth and sing the praises of the Lord. There were many different answers. One monk who was shooting pool had said nothing and when asked what he would do, he looked up and said, "I'd keep playing billiards!" Surely, the others said, that would be blasphemous! "Not at all," he replied, "because if I am a different person playing pool than I am in church or in the fields, then I am not the man I want to be. It is my intention that in everything I do, I do it all with love and appreciation. I want every moment of my life to be a living prayer of thanks!"

In the best, truest sense, that is living an authentic life.

ABOUT
MAX HOWARD

*M*ax Howard is a coal miner's son, raised in the mountains of Eastern Kentucky in a place called Snake Hollow. Considered a gifted student with a brilliant future, he became a professional actor and won television's coveted Emmy Award. He now works with business people who want to maximize performance by returning authenticity to their personal and professional lives. He lives in Atlanta.

Contact Information:
Max Howard
Max Howard Associates
429 Rays Road
Stone Mountain, GA 30083
Phone: (404) 296-8963
Fax: (404) 294-0670
E-mail: Max@MaxSpeaks.com
www.MaxSpeaks.com.

THE 5-P JOURNEY
FROM 4-F TO TRIPLE-A

by Charlene Lockwood, M.A.

Did you ever stand on the edge of forever? On the edge of the ocean and hear the songs of yesterday, today, and tomorrow in the rhythm of the waves? Have you ever walked a beach many times before you really walked the beach? Have you ever been filled with the immensity of a moment? Have you ever experienced moments of wholehearted success?

Wholehearted Success — enthusiastic, energetic, sincere effort to a favorable termination of attempts — is not in thunderous waves of applause; is not in checks for large fees; is not in bank accounts, stocks, jewelry, houses. Wholehearted success comes from *The 5-P Journey from 4-F to Triple-A.*

What are *4-F and Triple-A*? A military term used during the days of the draft, *4-F* meant unfit to serve. It did not mean something was radically wrong: rather, it meant someone was unfit to participate with others in the rigors of military life. There was something unacceptable about the individual. The *4-F* rating often left a deep scar on the mind, with accomplishments easily forgotten. *Triple-A* meant the top of the crowd, to be authentic, achieving, accepted.

As a teen, I received many opportunities and achieved success. But at 14 I did not associate the first place in a speech contest and a subsequent television appearance, as validations of writing and speaking ability. When 16, I did not connect receiving a National Science Foundation Scholarship to study at the University of Chicago as a validation of intelligence. At 17, I did not link the First Place Award at a State Music Competition as a validation of talent, nor did I comprehend the significance these events would have for my future.

Ability, intelligence, and talent did not mean being above the crowd or as good as the crowd; they meant being different. Different. *4-F*. Ability, intelligence, and talent meant little. I discounted them since significant role models in my life at that time also diminished them. I was *4-F* in a *Triple-A* world and I longed to be *Triple-A*: Authentic, Achieving, Accepted.

I did not understand the process that made each of the accomplishments possible and would eventually lead to my wholehearted success. The *5-Ps* — Picture, Purpose, Possibilities, Persistence, Patience — made each accomplishment possible. I did not start with the idea of appearing on television. Rather, I wanted to fit in with peers by doing what they were doing. I did not begin with the idea of attending the University of Chicago. Instead, I wanted to please a high school science teacher. I did not start with the idea of a State Music first place award. I wanted to delight a high school music teacher and a dying piano teacher. In each case, I began with my picture of being accepted. That was the image. That was the beginning of the accomplishments. While that was the vision for those fulfillments, other pictures were also there. I wanted to be successful. I wanted to be beautiful. I wanted it all!!

The picture became the model for my future manifestations. That representation begins the *5-P Journey from 4-F to Triple-A*.

The Picture

In 1987 the minor dents and scratches in my 22-year marriage were reaching enormous proportions. I was truly *4-F*. I was over forty, fat, fearful, and female in a young, slender, confident, and male-dominated business world. I had spent over 25 years developing wifely, motherly, domestic skills. The things I did — starting groups for the benefit of children, nurturing, giving, sharing from my abundant learning — were all done with the sole purpose of being respected and accepted, of being *Triple-A*.

The possibility of being a single mom with four children at home and only domestic skills grew, and reality slapped me. Someone asked me, "What do you want?" and I could not answer. Another asked the same question. Then another. I had no idea. "When you were younger, what did you want to be?" and I still could not answer. The conversation in my mind began:

"What do you want?"

"I don't know."

"When you see yourself in 30 years, what do you see?"

"Me? Probably dead."

"What is the picture?"

"What picture?"

"Envision what you want."

"What I want? I don't know. No one has ever asked what I want."

"Then, picture yourself knowing what you want. What might it look like, if you knew what you wanted?"

"What would I look like if I knew what I wanted?"

"Yes. What might you be like — confident? Skydiving? Writing a book? Getting an education? What would you be doing? Would you be waiting for the tide to bring you good things, or would you swim to meet the tide?"

As a personal coach, I often ask my clients to answer the same question, "What do you want?" This is as difficult a question for them to answer as it was for me. As children we are taught to be interested in another's welfare first: take care of your little sister or brother, be kind, share. Good boys and girls do that. That's the way to get along with others, to be liked, to be accepted. Stand up for yourself, but do not create problems doing so. Do well in school. Make good grades. This learning sets a pattern for the rest of life: caring for and being kind to others, taking turns, and sharing. This is the pattern to achieve goals that may not be ours, or the way we would do things. We will do it over and over, wanting to be accepted, and we slowly drain our well of dreams.

We know that if a person's well is dry, nothing is left to take care or be kind with, or share. We are empty and we are the image of what we don't want. Visualize yourself taking care of and being kind to you. Conceive of you, taking a turn and sharing with yourself. Create in your mind the "what if . . ." and the "what if not . . ." Envision the impossible. Dream the difficult. Imagine the unimaginable. Picture — the time to bring into focus the dreams, desires, and dementia. It is a picture you can have. Think of the musical *South Pacific*, when Bloody Mary sings, "If you don't have a dream, how you gonna have a dream come true?"

Often we are told to get our heads out of the clouds, to do instead of dream, to participate instead of picturing. Picturing, the dreaming and visioning, is not a selfish thing. It is a kind thing, a giving thing. When you do this for yourself, you can do it for others. So, find a quiet place, wherever you feel safe and peaceful, and let your mind be free. You will find many quiet places when you seek one. It does not matter if it is a large city like Phoenix, Arizona, or a small one like Rapid City, South Dakota, there are quiet spots. I have found quiet on mountain and tundra, beach and desert, forest and park, and in the heart of big cities. Where might you find quiet in a bustling city? One place is in a cemetery filled with peace and quiet. Summer and winter bird songs will trill past your thoughts allowing the mind to roam free to create what your heart desires. Think of other places you might find quiet.

Find your quiet or sacred place. Allow yourself to dream. Make a note or two. Let the images come and go and change. View yourself in yesterday, today, and tomorrow. Make other notes and repeat this process frequently. When we are able to picture ourselves knowing what we want, we begin to uncover the second P — Purpose.

The Purpose

Purpose is the reason for the want! What is the commitment that leads to motivation for the picture I have in my mind? What is it about this picture and not another? What is important in this scene? What are the reasons for doing the things you see in your mind? Do you want them for financial success? To show the world you are someone important? To share with the world? To be a leader? To teach? To invent? To explore? To influence one individual to become the "more" they dreamed of when they were younger? Or, something else more personal to you.

David O. McKay, a great ecumenical leader, said, "Find a purpose in life so big that it will challenge your every capacity to be your best." This is the beginning of a love affair with yourself. This is the beginning of giving yourself Mark Twain's belief, "I have not done a day's work in my life, for should it have been work, I would not have done it." When we are able to discover the purpose that is uniquely ours, we can be challenged at each moment and it doesn't seem like work. It is then that "work" becomes a passion and a joy.

How will you discover your purpose? Begin now by making three lists. This is one of the first exercises my coaching clients do. I ask them to make one list of 100 positive things people say about them. Some are tangible: for example, great cook, fabulous proofreader, fixes engines and knows what makes them really work well! And others may be intangible: for example, excellent listener; encouraging of others; kind to everyone; intelligent; well read. My clients balk at first and continue to press on. This is the first step to discovering purpose.

Next, make a second list of 100 things you admire in others, that is, those attributes, values, gifts, or whatever it is you value in them. For me, I admired the elegance of women like Loretta Young, Audrey Hepburn, and Grace Kelly. I knew nothing of their personal lives; however, I considered them elegant. I respected the writings of Chiam Potok, Ella Wheeler Wilcox, and Elizabeth Barrett Browning. I was fascinated by the speaking ability of John F. Kennedy, Winston Churchill, and Martin Luther King, Jr. What do you admire in others? Once you notice, you will be empowered in yourself with what you admire in others.

The third, final list is 100 things you are good at or like to do. Do your lists have to contain 100? No, they may have more than 100; however, stopping before the final thoughts come out may mean missing some of the best parts of yourself. Therefore, I recommend making the lists as long as possible. Do set a time limit, or you may be writing and never get to the purpose you are seeking.

Now, look at what you have written. What are the similarities? What are the opposites? Do they appear on the same list? Between lists? Where do the lists overlap? What do others see you as good at doing that you love to do? What do you enjoy doing that others do not see? Find the overlaps and gaps.

The next step is to compile these items in a way that groups them and makes sense to you. Consider them further and discover commonalities. You will find clarity when you narrow the many to a more comfortable number and develop a statement that encompasses ownership.

For example, one of my clients, Elizabeth, had extensive entries on all the lists that contained things she did with her hands. In essence, she was admired for her beaded costumes, her jewelry-making, and her cooking, gardening, sewing. The *doing* was not what she liked the most. She enjoyed the *creating*. She used that insight to develop a statement about herself as follows: "I am creative." This was the first portion of her purpose statement, the reason to fulfill her picture of herself. Her completed statement said, "Using my creativity, I bring beauty to my life and the lives of others."

Another client, C.J., found that many comments on his lists pointed to his ability to distill vast amounts of information into a one- or two-sentence statement that provides laser focus to life's issues. His statement for this aspect of his picture is, "I am focused." At the same time, he found a love for creating things and declared, "I am creative." Today he is using these two statements of purpose to explore photography possibilities for his vision of personal success.

While this could be a work in progress for years for many who have strayed, it is important to move forward with baby steps. (In my case I went through many iterations of my picture statement before it became challenging and stretched me daily. The want remained constant as the statement evolved.)

When you have your statements — rough or refined — you are ready to move to the how — Possibilities, Persistence, and Patience.

The Possibilities

Possibilities! The word flows from tongues with an endless stream of feelings, thoughts, and actions. There is a lilt and an openness, lifting and encouraging the mind to move beyond the black and white of everyday events. Possibilities present the opportunity to review the reality of what was and what is and move to the unknown of what will be.

To begin this portion of your ongoing journey, take large sheets of paper and pens (crayons or magic markers will stimulate your mind with color) and launch your travel into the unknown. Begin writing or drawing any thought that comes to mind that lifts and encourages you toward your picture and purpose statements. Remember, there are no right or wrong answers. Instead, you have possibilities to make "the picture" a reality! Your ideas may seem to be from outer space. This does not matter. What matters here is to get as many ideas as possible onto paper as quickly as you can. This is not the time to judge them or to ask, "How could I ever do that?" It is the time to brainstorm and put on paper any and all possibilities. You can always eliminate later.

Okay. You have a spectacular list of possibilities, a montage of the mundane and the magnificent. "So what?" you may be asking. Now, the fun begins! Join the ideas with loops and weave a flower chain. Draw squiggles and say, "Too far out!"

Or, become linear and build an outline, or a time line with milestones. You choose. You accept for yourself. You accept what works for you. You may discard or put on the back burner for future consideration. Most importantly, YOU CHOOSE! When was the last time you felt you had choice? Here you can feel the joy and the power of choosing for yourself!

Elizabeth, the creative client I referred to, also discovered a love of learning and sharing. One of her possibilities included getting a college degree. At first blush, this appeared an impossible task because she was almost 60, had not completed high school, and had spent her entire adult life caring for others. Today, she has accomplished the first steps toward that likelihood: she has her GED and a year of college completed. In addition, her creativity in jewelry is gaining regional attention. Sometimes the attention is international when I wear pieces she creates.

For C.J., the focused, creative client, who also has great knowledge of history and loves solitude, the possibilities include using these as he travels, researches, and documents the research with photographs. He takes the photos and does research, and his friend writes the books. What a synergistic way to fulfill his picture and purpose!

How will you get from the choice to the *Triple-A*? First, begin where you are and don't stop until the picture seems real. Then, employ Persistence.

The Persistence

Persistence — the willingness to resolutely move forward on a chosen path regardless of obstacles. This is when the path from *4-F* to *Triple-A* becomes challenging. Suddenly, every probable and improbable barrier rises to confront the progress. This is a time when every word of negative self-talk screams, and the positive self-talk becomes an inaudible whisper. Now is the time to look at your picture, reaffirm your purpose, and press through the possibilities.

To accomplish this, begin with the small steps of the choice, the tiny things that bring success. For instance, the phone call you make to someone you admire in a company you'd like to work for may be empowering. Or, the online search for sources to learn more about a topic. Whatever the little thing is, build on it. Celebrate the accomplishment of the first, the second, and the third small triumph, until the larger task is completed. With each courageous, persistent, small triumph remember and celebrate it. Revel in it! Smile and savor the success! Own the accomplishment! Use that success to give greater courage to move past the next rock in your path — the discouraging word you hear — the frustration you feel. Use that success to give more positive words to your daily self-talk. It's about taking baby steps.

One important way to persist and to support yourself is to surround yourself with those who want to assist you. Many will observe and help you. They are the people you find in the most unlikely places — a meeting you attend by chance, a letter you answer, a simple kindness and then, the reward comes far beyond your wildest imagining. Sometimes that person could be in a line at the grocery store.

This happened to me. Three years ago, I was once again in a situation of changing my world. My youngest child was about to graduate from high school. My second marriage was repeatedly jarred with difficult situations. I didn't like what I was doing although I loved the company I worked for. Again, it was time to evaluate where I was and decide what I wanted. I had evaluated in 1987 and set goals, but I had not developed a picture and purpose statement that would inspire, stretch, and fulfill me for the rest of my life. I had not looked at possibilities beyond the immediate need.

The company I worked for was undergoing a merger. I had heard the word "coaching" bantered about as assisting those in upper management to bridge the transitions required by the merger. I was in transition and thought it might help me to move forward more gracefully. In a grocery line at 11:30 p.m. the Tuesday before Thanksgiving a few years ago, I met Margie Summerscales. I looked over at her and asked, "What are two nice women like us doing in a grocery store at this time of night?" Mind you, we weren't even at the same counter. In spite of that, we began a conversation and exchanged business cards. Margie is a personal and executive coach. She later became my coach and assisted me in developing my picture and purpose.

Since that night, Margie and I have partnered and worked together. She introduced me to people in an entirely different industry that have assisted me to be where I am today. Today she supports me as I persist in bringing my dreams and possibilities to reality. Many times the world and picture seemed very bleak. I would make a decision and only trouble came.

People like Margie will ask you the right questions. They will not solve your problems for you, nor will they do your work for you. Instead, they will offer possibilities, insights, and observations. They will share how they did something similar and how it made their lives easier. They will show you doors you never expected were there and help you see them. They will not open doors; rather, they will encourage you to open them.

These people are mentors and coaches who will support you as you persevere in attaining your picture and living your purpose. They are the encouraging ones. They make observations and rely on you for your brilliance in discovering the best solution.

I had the picture. I had the purpose. But, I had times when my world seemed doomed to total destruction. I knew from experience the solutions were inside me.

At one of the blackest moments, when everything said I could not get beyond the mountainous challenge without help, I attended a local speakers' meeting. I hoped to discover an opening to my next step to fulfilling my dream. There I met Marsha Petrie Sue.

Marsha was in charge of a project and wanted help. She said it was part of her purpose to give to others more than she received from them. And, she delivered more than I have ever dreamed. As we worked on the project, Marsha asked questions and learned my dreams. She pointed me to the door of a major seminar company and gave me a name. She mentioned me to the individual that I would be auditioning for and gave me pointers for the audition. The rest was up to me. Guess what? I got the position!

You will too! Persist in your possibilities for your picture and purpose. Be patient with yourself, for it is your primary key and lifeline.

The Patience

Patience — the ability to be steadfast to your picture and purpose when everything and everyone "out there" says it won't happen.

Persistence is to move resolutely forward at the darkest moments. Patience is to hold the picture and light firmly when you perceive darkness. These two, along with the multitude of possibilities, are the how of going from *4-F* to *Triple-A*. Patience is holding fast to the dream. It is also bearing the burden of discouragement and dispiriting comments from those whose opinions you may value. Patience is being steadfast to the higher "yes" inside and the ability to say "no" to everything that does not support your picture. Patience is also saying something I coined many years ago, "A lapse in my behavior does not mean I have given up my standards."

I have discovered many roads lead to the goal. Persistence says, "Keep going" to the individual struggling to cross the finish line. Patience says "Yes" to the dream of finishing when everything says "No." Patience says, "Be still in this moment" when everything says activity will accomplish something. Patience says, "Hold the course" when bankruptcy is all you can see. Patience is remaining steadfast to the picture.

In an Iron Man competition in Kona, Hawaii, two women fell just feet from the finish line. Their legs were spent, but the dream persisted. Repeatedly each tried to stand. Then they sat patiently hoping to find a way to finish the race. They did. They crawled the distance to complete their picture.

When I first began in 1987 as the *4-F*, over forty, fat, fearful, female, I had no idea the accomplishments of my youth would have such a huge impact! The writing, the speaking, the intelligence, and the music have all played roles in who I am and what I do today. Many other pictures also emerge. Multiple purposes are being fulfilled. And the possibilities are endless. The persistence to move forward and the patience to be still (the quieting of mind) add daily to the richness of my *Triple-A* life.

Most important — What is your picture? What is your purpose? What are the possibilities for you? What might be the challenges? How will you persist through and beyond them? Who will encourage and support? What will you do when your patience is strained to breaking? What do you see when you stand on the edge of forever? What are you committed to for making your *5-P Journey from 4-F to Triple-A*?

ABOUT
CHARLENE LOCKWOOD, M.A.

Charlene Lockwood is an author, speaker and trainer, and personal coach whose purpose is "to use her enthusiasm, intelligence, and abundant gifts to encourage, empower and exalt humanity." In her work as a speaker and trainer she draws on her experiences in the computer, financial, and training industries. As a personal coach, she employs the same common sense approaches that worked when guiding her five children to adulthood. The grandmother of eight, Charlene believes there is choice in everything — even in chosing between doing something with happiness or sadness. She combines her experience, knowledge, high energy, and humor to give participants thought-provoking, fun, interactive learning designed to assist them in composing their picture and living their purpose.

Contact Information:
Charlene Lockwood, M.A.
NMX Inc.
P.O. Box 66805
Phoenix, AZ 85082
Phone: (602) 524-4354
Pager: (888) 506-4499
E-mail: CKLockwood@msn.com

LEAD BY EXAMPLE

by D.J. Harrington, CSP

To me, success is not a destination; it's a journey. First things first. Have fun on your journey. Let me begin where I think success starts, when we are young.

Success Begins at a Young Age

So often during seminars across the country, I have a chance to tell humorous things that happen. One night while on the road, I called home. My wife Sheila told me about a package that I had received in the mail. I told her to go ahead and open it. As she did she said, "Oh, my! There's a can and it looks like it has eyes all over it. Who would have sent you such a thing?" I answered, "Oh, honey, that is an 'Eye Can'." She wasn't as concerned about receiving a prototype of an eye can as she was that I had been telling my audiences about the incident. "You haven't been telling people about the 'eye can' have you?" she said accusingly. More for my defense, "Yes," I responded proudly because I had been telling audiences for the past couple years about what happened to us. Now let me tell you what prompted Sheila's concern.

Success Secrets That Children Tell: Developing An "I Can" Attitude

I came home late one Friday evening to find a note that read, "Mr. D.J. Harrington." As I opened it, I realized it was from my daughter's first grade teacher. My six-year-old daughter, Erin, was attending Boston Elementary School. The teacher was asking me to call her during the weekend to set up an appointment to meet with her the next week. Well, because I was leaving Sunday night to go back on the road, there wasn't any way I could accommodate her.

I called the teacher, explained that I was Erin Harrington's dad, and asked her if there were any possible way to discuss this problem over the telephone. "On, no, . . . we have to meet," she said. Her comment signaled a major infraction. Later that night, I asked Erin if she might have done anything in school during the week that would generate a note from the teacher. Her comeback was something like, "Dad, she wrote the letter to you . . . maybe you did something wrong!" It's like they say, "The fruit doesn't fall far from the tree." When I asked my wife why she hadn't read the letter, she politely told me that it was addressed to D.J. Harrington, and, "Dear, that's you."

On Saturday, I connected again with the teacher by phone, but she insisted on an appointment Sunday afternoon at the school. After church, my wife and I went to the school where we saw the principal's car in the parking lot, alongside an unfamiliar automobile.

The principal kindly unlocked the door for us, and we meandered down to Erin's classroom while making small talk. We took our seats on small chairs indigenous to a classroom of six-year-olds with our knees pressed to our chests. Then we started to discuss what had happened that Tuesday while I was traveling. My daughter was involved in a notorious spelling bee — a classical test of boys against girls! The teacher described the background, detailing that the girls stood up, and my daughter proceeded to the line. The teacher stopped her story and asked me if I had ever been in a spelling bee. I looked at the lady and said, "Ma'm, get to the chase . . . what did my daughter do?" She said, "In a spelling bee, Mr. Harrington, you have to say the word, spell the word, and then say the word again. If you are correct, then you proceed back to the end of the line."

"Okay, Mrs. Warren, I've been in a spelling bee before." With knitted eyebrows, I questioned her, "What happened?"

She replied, "Your daughter was next in line, and her word to be spelled was *can't*. I asked Erin to please spell the word CAN'T. Your daughter looked at me with sternness and hands on her hips, and said, "That word is not in my vocabulary. I'm not allowed to say the word." The teacher told me her mouth dropped open, and she asked Erin, "What? Who told you that?"

"My daddy," Erin said. "Can I write it on the board?"

So, Erin went to the front of the classroom and did just that. The teacher then instructed Erin to go to the end of the line as usual when the answer was correct. As Erin was walking to the back of the line, the teacher asked what her daddy does for a living. Erin told her that her daddy makes people feel good even if they feel bad.

Oh, brother! I guess she imagined that I sell drugs or something. I don't think that children really know what their parents actually do for a living. Much of my time is spent in airports, and if I had a little person at home now, she would probably think that I work at the airport.

Well, as she was going to the end of the line, Mrs. Warren said, "Erin has your father ever done anything else weird?" A helpful little girl offered, "Erin, tell the teacher about your dad!" When she was in kindergarten, I sat Erin down in our living room and gave her a pair of plastic scissors and Elmer's glue, and located and removed pictures of eyeballs from magazines and newspapers. We cut out Ronald Reagan's eyeballs, Margaret Thatcher's eyeballs, and bloodshot eyeballs of Willie Nelson. Every pair of eyeballs we found, we glued onto the side of a tin can.

The tin can was a large Campbell soup can perfect for eyeballs. I meticulously removed the soup label, and we glued the eyeballs to the side of the can until every inch of the can was filled with eyeballs. She brought the "eye can" in for Show and Tell and displayed it for everybody at the school. Erin was asked to go around and show it to every grade from kindergarten to sixth.

Today my daughter is a freshman in college and excels in tennis. One day someone asked her why she wears a certain pin and where did she get it. The pin reads, "Attitude is everything." She responds proudly, "I got it from my dad. My dad gave me the 'eye can' attitude."

"What does your dad do for a living?" Today, at age eighteen, she tells an interviewer that her father helps people develop from within, so they don't go without.

My wife was off to the side listening to this interview, and on the way home, she questioned Erin about her answer. "What do you mean, your dad helps people develop from within so they don't go without?" Erin interrupted her impatiently with "Mom . . . I listened to one of his videos!"

I'm going to tell you if you have little people in your family, you need to avoid, as much as possible, saying the word can't. However, at times adults may need to occasionally use can't, whether at work or when disciplining. If there are little people in your family, sit down, take out the plastic scissors, cut out eyeballs, and glue them to the side of the can.

Train them that as Americans they should always have an "I can" attitude. America wouldn't be where it is today if our forefathers had not developed an "I can" attitude. Let me ask you, is there an "eye can" in your life?

My dad's unusual props

One weekend, I asked my daughter Erin to help sell videos in the back of the auditorium after one of my speeches. She watched inquisitive people attending my classes ask questions about my unusual props. When they walk in the auditorium, take a swift sight inventory of my prop table, they see many things. One prop is actually a prospector's hat. Crowned with a big red light on the metal helmet, it is capable of illuminating a large portion of the auditorium as well as a cave, just as it was intended.

Do you create or extinguish fires?

My attendees recognize other props, such as the headgear of a train conductor and a fireman. One or two of the bravest attendees walk over and boldly ask, "Why all of these hats?" My answer . . . "Well, a lot of times we have to don a fire chief hat because, as managers, we usually extinguish fires." If you don't have a fire to put out, what do we normally do? That's right . . . we create one!

Through my travels and sales training studies across the United States, Australia, Canada, and the UK, I find there are many sizes and shapes of managers, and generally the only hat they know how to wear with expertise is the fire chief hat, and most of them think their team are arsonists.

Are you on the right track for success?

What hat are you wearing for success? Also on the prop table there are a train conductor's hat and a train whistle, which I purchased from a major toy company. When I blow the whistle, the whole room comes to attention as if I have just told the entire group, "All aboard, the train to success is leaving." That's when I relive my learning experience between Germany and France. The episode went like this.

It was four o'clock in the morning when the conductor came to get my ticket. As I rubbed the sleep from my eyes, I looked at this seasoned gentleman and located my American passport and rail pass and handed both to him as he had requested. Expressionless, he glanced at me and then at my credentials, and in broken English smothered with a French accent, he said, "Where are you going; where have you bEEn; and how are you going to get there?" My instincts told me that it really wasn't his business to know mine, especially at four o'clock in the morning.

I could still hear his words ring in my ears for miles down the track. Later, I would know how important his three questions would be.

Wouldn't that be a good message for me to carry back to the United States while donning conductor's hat and blowing a whistle? When speaking to audiences, I could ask where have we been, where are we going, and how are we going to get there. Are we on the right track? Are we going in the right direction? Have we taken too much baggage?

What hat are you wearing throughout the day?

There are times when a person who goes through divorce or alienation carries unnecessary baggage forever. This baggage could be from physical, emotional, or professional problems; regardless, he goes through life forever carrying past hurts on every trip. Every time I return from a trip, the first thing I do is unpack, or depending on how quickly I leave again, I weed out certain items I do not need for the next trip.

Am I going in the right direction? Do I have the proper ticket for the right trip? Sometimes I like to look down at the ticket I have purchased and see if the destination and the amount that I paid to board the train or plane were really worth it. I want to ask the same to you. How much are you willing to pay to reach your final destination? Are you willing to take time out to learn, to read, and listen so you can develop within so you don't go without?

Do you pray for success or work as if it depends solely on your efforts?

Further down my prop table, the attendees spot my priest hat. It was a cool day in spring spent running errands with my wife. I wanted an original priest hat. Sheila and I searched unwaveringly for a church supply store that had one in stock. Under the disapproving eye of the sales clerk, I bought the complete ensemble. I reassured the clerk that I was appearing as Father Carforu on the Automobile Satellite Training Network and needed the outfit for credibility. Without that explanation, I doubt she'd have sold it to us.

During this satellite segment, my bishop was known as Bishop U-Sell-i. The segment was well received, and I kept the hat. Father Carforu told managers that they should pray for some salespeople in their department; they needed it. That would cause my audience to laugh and joke around. It gave me an opportunity to create fun in the class, but, truthfully, I do believe we should have prayer, providence, and perseverance. Prayer changes; providence provides; and perseverance accomplishes.

Are you known for depressing or stifling the performance of others?

Next to the priest hat is another hat that looks like a Russian-Soviet winter hat. It is made of fur with flaps that can be untied to cover the ears. Reminiscent of uncompassionate faces of Russian soldiers, I call it my "stinking thinking" and "doom and gloom" hat. It's a depressing hat. Some people easily identify with the hat, because they, too, were weaned on a dill pickle and have hated their mothers since age three. Those people are really out there. Generally, a person who brightens up the whole department by leaving the room wears it.

Another one that I recognize is the Chevrolet hat or Caterpillar hat, or one of the hats from Mohawk Carpet, Damon or Cal Pro, and I wonder whether people realize it's not the cap or the garment that we cover ourselves with but what's inside that counts. It doesn't matter if we're wearing a hat with a logo that says "Tommy Hilfiger," "Genuine GM Parts," or "Federal Express." The final truth is what's inside.

Expecting an overweight individual to be a pole-vaulter seems an impossible feat. If I were a coach, my advice would be, "Just throw your heart over the pole, and the rest of your body will go with it."

Do you see disaster in everything or do you provide viable solutions?

The prospector's hat, which I mentioned earlier, is the last one on the prop table. Primarily the prospector's hat is used for mining caves. When I put that hat on, I hear gasps of "Oh, my! Where is he going with this?" Then I have an opportunity to tell them that it's similar to when I spoke to the disaster recovery group that responded to the Oklahoma City bombing several years ago. I use a similar story when speaking to groups such as Caterpillar, IBM, Damon Motor Home people or the disaster recovery group.

Recently, I had an opportunity to wear that hat again and share this story once more. We were in the middle of the ocean on a dark, rainy night and all of a sudden through the fog, there was a light. We immediately contacted the captain and said, "There is a light in our sea lane." The captain said, "Signal to it, and tell them to move." So we did just that; we signaled, "MOVE FROM OUR SEA LANE." This time the captain also instructed us to tell them, "We are the great Missouri, the largest ship in the fleet, move from our sea lane." So, we signaled that message . . . WE ARE THE MISSOURI, THE LARGEST SHIP IN THE FLEET, MOVE FROM OUR SEA LANE." The retaliatory message came swiftly . . ."WE ARE THE LIGHTHOUSE!"

Are you working toward success wherever you are?

So, my different hats project different scenarios to my audiences. In the last couple of years I have thoroughly enjoyed my Secret Recipes hat because I've seen many people accomplish much. All of us are a part of a secret recipe of success. You were kind enough to purchase this book and are reading it one-on-one as if I am sitting next to you. Before going on the next chapter, I want you to answer this question honestly.

What hat are you wearing? Are you wearing the fire chief hat putting out recurring fires, or are you wearing the priest hat — always praying for the situation? I heard one man tell me he kneels down to pray, knowing it depends on God, and then works relentlessly like it all depends on him. That's when you'll be truly blessed.

Don't be like the person who gets motivated, runs around his house, sings in the shower, does all the affirmations, and then goes back to bed. What hat are you wearing in life?

Check List for Leaders

- Be a positive example for your children and others in everything you do.
- Develop an "I can" attitude for yourself. Project that attitude to others.
- Do not create fires; learn to extinguish them quickly and effectively.
- Choose the right path for yourself; don't rely on others to show you the way.
- Make sure you wear the appropriate hat when dealing with people.
- Recognize disaster as an opportunity to provide viable solutions.
- Do not stifle creativity whether yours or others. Offer positive support.
- Analyze what it will take to make you successful and spend 15 minutes each day working toward that goal.
- Pray for your success, but get off your knees and work as if everything depends solely on you.

Garden for Success

By D.J. Harrington

FIRST PLANT
7 ROWS OF PEAS

- Presence
- Promptness
- Preparation
- Patience
- Perseverance
- Positive Action
- Prayer

THEN PLANT
8 ROWS OF SQUASH

- Squash Gossip
- Squash Indifference
- Squash Indecision
- Squash Negativity
- Squash Worry
- Squash Envy
- Squash Greed
- Squash Fear

THEN PLANT
9 ROWS OF TURNIPS

- Turn-up for Training
- Turn-up On Time
- Turn-up With a Smile
- Turn-up With Good Thoughts
- Turn-up With New Prospects
- Turn-up With Excitement
- Turn-up With a Positive Attitude
- Turn-up With Determination to Make Everything Count for Good

NO GARDEN IS COMPLETE WITHOUT LETTUCE

- Let Us Be Faithful to Our Duty
- Let Us Be Honest With Ourselves
- Let Us Be Unselfish and Loyal
- Let Us Be True to Our Obligations
- Let Us Have Fun and Enjoyment
- Let Us Obey the Rules and Regulations
- Let Us Love and Help One Another

AND LAST BUT NOT LEAST, LET'S ASK FOR GOD'S HELP.

ABOUT
D.J. HARRINGTON, CSP

D.J. Harrington, CSP is President of Phone Logic, Inc., an international telemarketing and training company based in Atlanta, GA. He serves as a consultant to over 600 businesses throughout the U.S. D.J. appears every week on ASTN, the national cable training network. Programs focus on prospecting to in-coming calls. As a syndicated columnist for 33 newspapers and Power Source *magazine, D.J. writes monthly articles that appear from Atlanta to Los Angeles. He is known as Mr. Motivator at General Motors, and by many of his clients as the Gallagher of the speaking circuit. His years as sales trainer and motivator for a variety of companies have provided D.J. with a diverse background which he combines with energy and his dynamic personality to provide memorable presentations for companies such as UniRoyal, General Motors, American Bank Systems, Bloomingdale's, IBM, American Express, Mohawk Carpet, Damon Motor Homes, Auto Services, Inc. and The Original On-Hold Company. D.J. is a member of the National Speakers Association and has earned their Certified Speaking Professional designation.*

Contact Information:
D.J. Harrington, CSP
Phone Logic, Inc.
2820 Andover Way
Woodstock, GA 30189
Phone: (770) 516-7796
Fax: (770) 516-7797
E-mail: DJHarrington@mindspring.com
Website: www.DJHarrington.com

HEART TO HEART: SEVEN KEYS FOR REDUCING STRESS AND CREATING A BALANCED LIFESTYLE

by Sharon A. Baker

W hy does it take losing a job, the death of a father, a change in location, or a terminal diagnosis from a doctor on a routine office visit to teach us the "heart" of living?

I am not a famous person. You do not know me. In fact you have never heard of me, yet you know me very well, for I am you. You are me. My story is your story.

Let's talk heart to heart if only for a chapter. Some might dismiss me for speaking so keenly of the heart. There lies the essence or pulse of any business. If I were to take the pulse of your business or career, at what rate would it be beating?

The Problem

I sometimes allow my emotions to talk for me. Sarcasm. Having to have the last word. Or overly responding to criticism. Are you relating? My body language is a dead giveaway. I like to make people, places, and outcomes respond to my demands. I believe any good therapist would identify me as a "controller." If only they would _____ then I would feel _____. Is this a familiar scenario? Am I alone?

Would you like to know what the secret to managing stress is? The secret is *get skilled*. Yes, be willing to get skilled at what you do not do well. Are you ready to look at what you don't do well? If so, I can assist you. Stress has become a buzzword in our society today, therefore stress gives me permission to blame others at the workplace for not treating me the way I think they should. If my kids would _____ then I would feel _____. If they only know how hard I worked at this job. I love teaching this seminar because in helping you I am helping me. Do you want to get better or bitter? How we choose to live our lives on a daily basis is the foundation for managing this creature called stress.

During a recent seminar I led in Orlando, Florida, a woman yelled back at me as I said the secret to managing stress is *get skilled*. She asked, "Did you say, '*get killed*?'" I responded with, "Honey, we *do* get killed every time we aren't willing to look at what we do not do well." We kill ourselves mentally, physically, emotionally, and spiritually both on and off the job. Self-esteem is lowered, anger rises, depression fogs our thinking, and emotions are over-emphasized. Thus the company we work for and the family we live with begin to spiral downward due to our inability to function at our peak. Yet, we live in our denial and say *if you had my job, if you were raising the kids I am, if you had to commute this far, if you sacrificed like I do, if your customers treated you like* — ad infinitum. Who cares to admit this truth: I am the reason I am stressed out!

I had to laugh when I thought about this the other day. Tell me if you can relate. I woke up late and was frantically preparing for a meeting. While driving in traffic to a client's company, I was angry at how slow some people were driving. I became so irritated, I wanted to send a hand signal to the driver in front of me on the freeway but stopped myself, thinking of the ramifications, laughed at myself (which is hard for me to do whenever I have reached this level of impatience) and said to myself, *why don't you tell the driver in front of you that you are mad at him for driving so slow because you got up late!* What a concept! Imagine. Need I say more? Yes, I like to blame others.

Is it stress or is it . . .

Insecurity, fear, anger, guilt, poor communications, sadness, or loneliness? Stress becomes the word I use instead of learning to get skilled at what I am not good at. How many of you have ever gone to a doctor and received a prescription for assertive communication skills? Can you take an MRI and have your level of anger and fear measured? Will your "blood count" determine the type of guilt you feel flowing through your arteries because you were late having dinner with your family as a result of the business meeting that ran past 5:00 p.m.? Can we put you on a doctor's scale to weigh the amount of loneliness you feel since your department was downsized and the friends you have made at ABC company have moved on to other departments, organizations, or cities?

Stress is good, believe it or not. Stress is needed for you and me to function at our maximum. Stress is bad once we become hostile. What are you hostile about?

Can I help you to discover some possibilities? Example: If he/she loved me he/she would _____. Why can't my boss read my mind? Can't my boss see I don't have the time? Why do my customers expect me to be available for them 24 hours a day? Can't he/she see I am afraid to speak my viewpoint when asked about this project in the presence of my staff? Are you still willing to look at what you do not do well? I am. I am willing to guide you as well as be guided by you. Let's do it.

The Consequences

People must remain teachable before they are reachable. Have we reached something together? What is it? Take a moment to write out what you would like to be taught.

Why does it take a wake-up call to make us teachable? Why do we have to have a tragedy in our lives to make us appreciate the precious gift we have called living for today?

This morning, I made my annual visit to the eye doctor. I am 47 years old and my eyes are changing. I complain about the nuisance that my bifocal contact lenses cause me at night while driving. My friend, Sam who is 76 years old, waits patiently at his apartment at the retirement center for a friend to drive him to the store to grocery shop.

How would I view my life if I suddenly became stricken with permanent lack of vision in both eyes? For me, the heart of my stress beats at the rate of my attitude. How fast does your attitude "beat" during times of stress? Our lives, wouldn't you agree, can be divided into four basic areas: *job, health, home and fun.* Some of us used to be fun. Some of us used to have a personal life. I have strong values. One of my strongest values is spending quality time with my family and friends. Yet, I work late at the office and give the people I value the most in my life leftover energy. I must be careful to check my personal values before I continue to check the values of my employer.

We become skilled at denying our core values and beliefs. We set ourselves up for failure (stress) by looking outside of ourselves for an easier way to eliminate the pain of stress, thus creating more stress in the form of broken relationships, late appointments, missed days from our jobs, and, in some cases, harmful addictions. Frustrated, we see no way out! Poor productivity, high medical costs, not to mention the broken spirit of a once carefree human being. Have you found yourself becoming a human *doing* instead of a human *being*? Do yourself a favor, write thoughtfully about these feelings for a moment — guilt, frustration, anger.

Baseball bats down, please. What do I mean by the baseball bat? The one you carry around with you to work and put on your bedside table every night. The baseball bat you use to beat yourself up with because you are not in perfect control of all aspects of your job, home, health, and fun. Negative self-talk, perfectionism, over-committing myself, and lack of proper rest. These are the demons or what I prefer to call them is the "itty, bitty stinking committee." The voices that sound in our heads like the stories Stephen King writes. Let's examine them for a brief moment. I didn't return all of my calls on my callback list today, therefore I must not be efficient. My kids didn't do so well in school this last semester, I must be a poor parent. My lawn wasn't mowed this weekend because I watched the big game, therefore, I must be lazy. I think the customer must not be pleased with my product because he didn't tell me so. My career isn't moving rapidly towards the promotion I seek, obviously I must no longer be promotable in the eyes of my organization. My marriage is not as exciting as it once was, does this mean we must be headed for divorce court? The itty bitty stinking committee tells you to change jobs or move to a better neighborhood without admitting the possibility that new situations can be as stressful as the old.

The Solution

My best friend, Sandy, often reminds me that I am either part of the problem or part of the solution. What choice are you willing to make with me? Here are the seven keys to reduce stress and create a balanced lifestyle.

Key 1: Create a Positive Disposition

"Baker, I have heard this before; have you forgotten? In other words, be positive." "No. I said, create." "Baker, I can barely create a safe path home while driving on the freeway in Monday night rush hour traffic after a full day of hard work and an angry customer who has been in my face all day. Don't tell me to think positive. At this point, I cannot think my way out of the supermarket shopping for dinner, much less create a positive disposition. Help me out, Sharon."

While driving home (or to the next hotel, in my case) I try to ponder these thoughts: What good has happened to me today? What little project did I complete? What customer was pleased today? When it is difficult, which sometimes it is, I will write down five blessings I have in my life as a result of my job. I can always find something good in a seemingly bad situation if I search hard enough; can you? Don't wait for the wake-up call to make you grateful. I lost my corporate position seven years ago at the age of forty and lived for one year unemployed. Why does it take a tragedy to make us stop and be grateful?

Key 2: Maintain Supportive Relationships

Where will I get the support I need if I am not constantly giving it in all my relationships, be they professional or personal? If I am busy giving all of my energy to my job, which is only one section of my life, who will maintain the other sections? I want my family and friends to know me intimately, and I bring home leftover energy. Leftover energy is not the energy that sustains supportive relationships. List the five most important people in your life:

1. _____

2. _____

3. _____

4. _____

5. _____

Did you put yourself on this list? I hope so.

How much quality time have I devoted to each person this past week? Is there a realignment due? How can I restructure my week to add the quality time necessary to nurture this relationship? Do I have enough self-esteem to terminate relationships that are not good for me? Is this relationship feeding me? Have you noticed that we prioritize our lives according to what we value the most? At the end of a busy workday, we frantically pack leftover energy with the reports to take home. Suggestion: Repack your briefcase!

Key 3: Encourage Others and You Will Encourage Yourself

It fascinates me how much better I feel at the end of a stress-packed day when I take personal note as to how I was able to be of service to someone other than myself.

My brother, Johnny, taught me this lesson. He was lying connected to a ventilator, breathing for his life, as he slowly succumbed to the disease of AIDS. My brother had me come into intensive care with my seminar props and rehearse a seminar on telephone skills at his bedside. Johnny couldn't tell me verbally how I did during my presentation, but he wrote his review on a sheet of paper. Johnny gave during a time in his life when others (like me) would have been thinking *what is in this for me*? I believe on that cold Chicago night, in the intensive care unit, John and I both encouraged each other to follow our destiny!

Two months later, my brother and friend, John J. Brzycki, Jr., died in his sleep, and my career as a professional speaker began. Thanks, Johnny, for the encouragement. I love you!

Key 4: Say What You Mean and Mean What You Say

It is hard to say "NO." Let's see how assertive you are.

Passive people allow others to violate their rights. They suffer from low self-esteem and will not communicate their needs to others because of fear.

Aggressive people violate the rights of others based on the same premise as the passive communicator.

Assertive people talk professionally and personally from a position of high self-esteem and confidence and acknowledge both the rights of self and others in their conversations.

PASSIVE   ASSERTIVE   AGGRESSIVE

Which are you? Place an X on the above scale that best describes the way you communicate at your job.

Now, place an O on the same scale that describes the way you communicate in your home. Do you consider yourself a person who says what you mean, and do you mean what you say?

Key 5: Take Control Instead of Being Controlled

Whom can we control? Ourselves! Invest in yourself. Upgrade your current professional skills. Remain teachable. Create written goals that you review daily. Listen to motivational and inspirational tapes. Take a class. Play that instrument you have wanted to learn how to play but have yet to make the time. (Like the golf pro I haven't hired yet to teach me how to play golf. The clubs are in the garage for the winter so next spring . . .)

Can you change the world? No. Can you make a difference? Always!

Key 6: Practice a Program of Spiritual Fitness

This is personal. My daily behavior, disposition, and attitude are contingent upon my spiritual fitness. How spiritually fit are you these days? I have a simple prayer that I meditate on before every seminar. It reads like this: "God, let me not be driven today by my ego or my greed. Let me be used by You to give them what You think they need. Amen."

Key 7: Respond to One's True Call at Work

People basically require a purpose in their lives: human connection beyond e-mail, voice mail, and snail mail. A life with substance and value. They need inspiration, encouragement, and a sense they have made a definite difference.

For many years I allowed others to control my future, make my decisions, determine my level of knowledge and all I did in return was blame "them." I thought for years I was a responsible person, yet I did not take responsibility for my decisions whenever I blamed others. Are you blaming or responding? Respond to the daily events in our lives that we call stress. Learn to get skilled at what you do not do well. Manage your stress or soon your stress will manage you!

God bless.

ABOUT
SHARON BAKER

*C*ombining a wealth of practical knowledge with high energy and creative problem-solving skills, Sharon Baker has won praise as a creative, dynamic speaker. Her winning attitude motivates participants and guides them to become more effective and productive professionally and personally. With over 10 years of experience in training and education, Sharon has developed additional expertise in time management, communication, sales, and emotional control skills. Her diverse client list includes Eli Lilly, Merck, Chiquita Brand and Teletouch.

Sharon stays current as a member of the National Association of Female Executives, Authors Guild, National Speakers Association and Toastmasters International.

Contact Information:
Sharon Baker, President
Let's Talk . . . RESULTS, inc.
2790 Paso Del Norte Drive Suite #1
Indianapolis, IN 46227
Phone: (317) 859-1214
Fax: (317) 859-1215
E-mail: Queene412@aol.com

You Too Can Be A Star In The Five Most Important Areas of Your Life

by Chet Marshall

"This necklace is perfect," I said to my wife as we stared inside the jewelry case. There was a beautiful silver necklace shaped like a star, outlined with small diamonds, in a beautiful wooden box, and it was called the "Millennium Star." How appropriate, I thought; my daughter Jennifer is a star to me, a bright and shining star, and I know she'll love it.

My wife and I were at our third port of call, on our two-week millennium cruise that would take us through the Panama Canal on New Year's Eve. I was determined to get Jennifer something special while on this trip, and the "Millennium Star" necklace was indeed perfect. We were on the lovely island of Aruba at our favorite jewelry store. My wife and I have been going to Aruba at least twice a year since 1993.

Six weeks later I was back in Aruba, and Jennifer was able to join me for a few days. It was my first opportunity to give her the necklace and she absolutely loved it. We had some very valuable one-on-one time and non-stop conversation. We covered topics from relationships, careers, religion, and politics to the general state of affairs. It was quality time that I as a father thoroughly enjoyed with my daughter. When I took her to the airport, she thanked me again for the necklace, and as she walked away, even through the mist of my eyes, the glow of my "star" daughter was apparent, at least to me.

The next day, some good friends of mine from Charleston, West Virginia came to spend a few days in our timeshare and check out Aruba. We had a great time of fellowship and conversations that covered a wide spectrum. I shared with them Jennifer's visit and the gift of the "Millennium Star" necklace. Part of our conversation centered on the condition of the world and how we felt the breakdown of relationships and in major areas of responsibilities was to blame for where mankind is today. Selfishness, greed, and the lack of integrity, trust, character, caring, commitment, patience, compassion, and respect all contribute to the breakdown.

That night, alone in my condo, I once again thought of Jennifer's visit, and the "Millennium Star" with its five points seemed to be tattooed to my eyelids. At each point I saw an important area of our lives that we need to strive to be stars in. If we strive to be stars in these five areas, we will make a better world for all mankind. Here's what I saw:

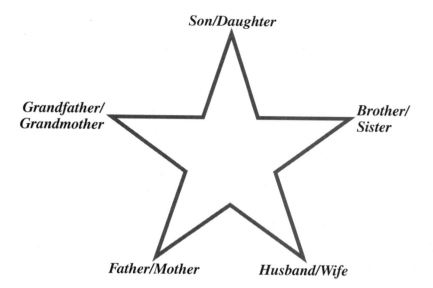

Son/Daughter

Grandfather/ Grandmother

Brother/ Sister

Father/Mother

Husband/Wife

I climbed out of bed, grabbed my pen and notebook, and started writing some of my thoughts. If these are the five most important areas of our lives, what are the five most important qualities we must possess to be a star in each of these areas? Everyone wants to be a star, but being a star in these areas of our lives is far more important than being a star actor, athlete, musician or any other lofty position given star status. We can all be stars in the five most important areas of our lives, and this star status is second to none in anything else we may achieve in life.

Being a star means being the best at whatever you are. Michael Jordan is a star because he's the best. Tiger Woods is a star because he's the best. Julia Roberts is a star because she's the best. We too can achieve star status by being the best son/daughter, brother/sister, husband/wife, father/mother, grandfather/grandmother, but as with any star status, it takes hard work, determination, and perseverance. This star status is one that every man, woman, and child should reach for.

A few days after my "star" thoughts occurred, this scripture leaped off the page during my daily devotional. "Do everything without complaining or arguing, so that you may become blameless and pure, children of God without fault in a crooked and depraved generation, in which you *shine like stars* in the universe as you hold onto the word of life." Philippians 2:14-16

Let's look at each of the five areas in our lives in which we can "shine like stars" in the universe and, more importantly, in our own personal world. Our very first important area of responsibility when we come into this world is that of a child.

Son/Daughter

From the earliest recollection of my Sunday school years I remember being taught to "Honor your father and your mother." How simple it would be for all of us, as children of all ages, to be stars if we just followed this one simple command. In Ephesians 6:1-3 we're taught "children, obey your parents in the Lord, for this is right. Honor your father and mother, which is the first commandment with a promise; that it may be well with you and you may live long on the earth."

"That it may be well with you" — what a wonderful thought. How many times have we stood by a casket and have heard sons and daughters cry out in haunting regret for the lives they have lived, the lack of interest they've shown, the lack of respect they've given, and the lack of unconditional love returned to a parent? It doesn't need to be that way because you can be a star in this very important area of your life.

Obeying and honoring are the key words we learn at a very early age, and they do not change as we get older. When we live a life of integrity, show the respect that is deserved, demonstrate reliability, are committed to being sons and daughters by giving unconditional love to our parents, we not only honor them, we are stars.

My mother will soon be 80 and if you asked her if her son is a star son or her daughter is a star daughter, her reply would be an unequivocable yes. But, like most parents, she's very biased in her thoughts. Back in 1990 she gave me a plaque entitled: "An Admirable Man."

If a man is honest with others and with himself . . .
If he receives gratefully and gives quietly . . .
If he is gentle enough to feel and strong enough
  to show his feelings . . .
If he is slow to see the faults of others
  but quick to discover their goodness . . .
If he is cheerful in difficult times and modest in success . . .
If he does his best to be true to his beliefs,
  then he is truly an admirable man.

On the back of the plaque was this handwritten note:

My Dear Chester,

   This surely was made for you! In Psalms "Selah" is mentioned so often — meaning " Amen." All I can add is Amen, Amen, Amen.

   Love Ya & Many Prayers,
   Mother
   5/6/90

Yea, she thinks I'm a star son, but I also have striven to be a good son and keep the commandments I've been taught. The commands are so simple, and, if followed, the world could be a much better place for us all. "Selah."

Brother/Sister

The bond between brothers and sisters can be likened to a roller coaster, but the truth is the coaster never leaves the track.

I've seen it time and again, the brother/sister who fought like cats and dogs, tattled on each other, had a complete lack of respect for each other, made fun of each other as children and yet became bonded with crazy glue as they matured. "Be kindly affectionate to one another with brotherly love in honor giving preference to one another." Romans 12:10. Again, another simple command that can help us be star brothers and sisters.

Maturity is a great and necessary time of our lives when we turn from our childish ways and learn the true values of life. One of those values is our relationship with our siblings. It's sad today to see brothers and sisters that are rivals, that haven't spoken to each other for years, that harbor feelings of hatred for each other and have no desire to be around each other. I'm certainly not blinded to the fact that all brothers and sisters aren't perfect. But yet I truly believe more of them could have striven to perfection if the brotherly love we're commanded to give had been completely demonstrated.

When we live a life of integrity, show the respect that is deserved, demonstrate reliability (we can be counted on), are committed to being all we need to be, by giving unconditional love to our brothers and sisters, we not only have the relationship we long for, but we are stars.

One of the things that caused me to fall in love with my wife was her sincere compassion for her brother. Her brother is "special," with a psychotic disorder and mental handicap. She made it clear that if any thing happened to her parents, she felt the need to make sure her brother was well taken care of, at whatever sacrifice was necessary. The other three sisters all have this compassion not only for their "special" brother but for each other. As sisters they are truly stars by the lives they live and demonstrate.

Husband/Wife

He said, " I do." She said, " I do." Those two little simple words spoken, but more importantly, lived out, should be all we need to be stars as husbands and wives. The wedding vows, which are exchanged in a matter of minutes, should be the springboard to matrimonial stardom.

This very important area of our lives is the first area where we make a choice. In the first two areas those decisions are made for us. The choices we make in selecting our mates are usually made because we believe the chosen one is a star. Think about it. To fall in love one with the other through the courting stages, the other becomes a real star in our eyes. He's the one! She's the one! Who makes me shine like no one else can. We've chosen stars for our mates; now it's just a matter of helping each other to continue to shine.

How? By living the vows we've exchanged and continuing to treat each other as the stars we fell in love with. The I do's are simple. So is His command to us to "Love one another," and my favorite that I feel is true star power is "doing unto others what we would want done to us." This is truly a life of loving that fulfills our every need. It also provides a role model for others, including our children.

When we share integrity one with the other, share the respect each deserves, make reliability real, are committed to our vows, and love each other unconditionally, we are stars of matrimony.

Y2K has not been a particularly easy year for my wife and me. We've realized a tremendous downturn in some of our business ventures, as well as income, and had family crises and other stresses not normally dealt with. I've been quoting Mother Teresa a lot, who said, "God wouldn't give us more than we could handle; I just wish He didn't trust me so much." Through communication my wife and I have been supportive and understanding and have kept a positive outlook that has allowed our marriage smooth sailing instead of a choppy uncharted course. My wife's willingness to do whatever is necessary is why she's the star I fell in love with, and her star status never dims.

Father/Mother

Momma! Dada! Those are the words we anxiously await to hear regardless of how clear they are. The responsibility that comes with those two words is about as awesome as we can imagine. The unconditional love is inbred in each parent but sometimes we have to call upon our "tough" love, too. The love settings for parents are numerous, and during the child rearing years you will use every setting of the dial. The unconditional love is the setting for parents to reach star status. However, there are many other requirements along the way.

The command "train up a child in the way he should go and when he is old he will not depart from it" has stood the test of time. In today's environment, children have so many influences to take them off track it is imperative for parents to be involved in their lives totally. To be a part of your children's future you must be in their lives today. Truett Cathy, CEO of Chick-fil-A, says, "It's easier to build boys and girls than to mend men and women." What a tremendous responsibility!

As parents, if our children witness a life of integrity, respect between mother and father and for themselves, know they can count on us, a commitment to the family unit and experience unconditional love, then as parents we can be stars.

Jason, my son, gave me a real honor when he asked me to be his best man at his wedding. Even though as a father I wasn't always perfect, he made me feel like a star. The ultimate honor, however, is watching him father his two daughters. His key to being a star father is that "he's not too busy making a living that he forgets to make a real life for his daughters." To watch him and his wife Dyan, as father and mother, "bringing them up in the training and admonition of the Lord" (Ephesians 6:4) and giving them the top priority of their lives qualifies them as stars. "Time" is a savings bond that pays eternal interest, and as parents in today's world, "time" with your children makes you a star.

Grandfather/Grandmother

"Grandpa, can you make a noise like a frog?" "Well, I guess I can, but why?" "Cause, grandma said when you croaked we're all going to Disney World!" Grandchildren! Don't you just love them.

Recently, I was asked to provide the Grandparent's Day message at a church in Ohio. The title of my message was "Grandparenting — AARP." The AARP served as an acronym for Awesome, Awesome Responsibility and Power of Influence. It is in fact an awesome responsibility, and the power to influence those young lives should cause grandparents to strive to be star grandparents.

"If I knew having grandchildren was going to be so much fun, I would have had them first." We've all heard that statement before and perhaps some of you have even uttered those words. Why is that? I visited a friend in Phoenix who said he was amazed at the transformation of his father when the first granddaughter was born. He remembered as a boy, a father who was cold, firm and unemotional. Yet, when the granddaughter arrived, his father turned all goo-goo ga-ga. There was a "grandloving" that my friend never experienced as he was growing up.

Why do grandparents act that way? Part of the reason comes from the word "more." As grandparents we have more time, usually have more money, somehow develop more patience, and certainly have more wisdom. It's easy to spoil grandchildren with "more" because we don't have to deal with them on a daily basis.

Grandparents, impressionable eyes are watching you. We're commanded to "share the gift of the word of life I've placed in you. I've destined you to shine like the stars of the universe to those around you." Philippians 2:15.

"Grandparenting is about being. Being there for family, taking time for the special moments in a grandchild's life, taking time to listen, praising instead of pushing, comforting instead of criticizing, giving instead of getting and loving instead of lecturing. Remember taking time requires your presence." These are excerpts from *Hugs for Grandparents*, by Dr. Harry Keefauver. My addition is "being one of high integrity, being respectful of those around us, being reliable to all our family members, committed to our responsibilities and being loving unconditionally, we will shine like stars to our grandchildren as well as the universe."

Jordyn Rose and Emylie Jean are the impressionable eyes that are watching me. I realize what an awesome, awesome responsibility and power of influence I have. It's that reality that drives me to strive to be a star grandparent.

The Five Qualities

You can't undo what has been done, but you can do what is undone. You too can be a star in the five most important areas of your life. There are many qualities and characteristics one must possess to become stars in these areas of our lives. During my research five qualities kept rising to the top. My research consisted of talking with more than one hundred people of different ages and stages of life. The five star qualities that consistently were mentioned in each of life's categories were, Integrity, Respect, Reliability, Commitment and the greatest of these, Love. When people talked about love it was always mentioned as unconditional or "agape" love.

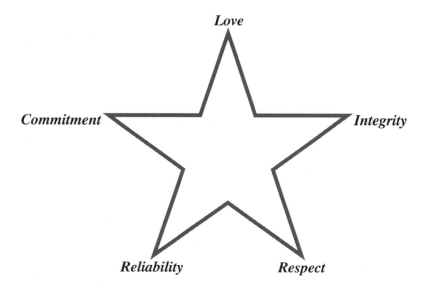

Integrity — Trust is the synonym of integrity. Trusting is such a vital part of a strong relationship. A person's word, actions, character are what we want to be able to "take it to the bank" and "believe it as gospel." Integrity is the steel beam that can't be bent, broken or twisted.

Psalm 26:1. "Vindicate me, O Lord, for I have walked in my integrity . . . I shall not slip."

Respect — The "respect" that is paid when someone has passed on is far better spent when that someone is still alive. In all areas of our lives the respect we have and give in our relationships should be the same respect we desire for ourselves.

Reliability — You can count on me to be there — when you need help, when you need someone to listen, when you are lonely, when you need to share a celebration, just whenever. There's a song that says "In the good times, in the bad times I'll be by your side forever more," but there's also a scripture verse that says, "I will never leave you nor forsake you." That's the reliability we need to emulate in our life's areas of responsibility.

Commitment — The marriage vows are the commitments we make between husband and wife and wife and husband. There's a ceremony with witnesses to those vows. As sons/daughters, brothers/sisters, father /mothers and grandfathers/grandmothers there are no ceremonies, no vows, just His commands and encouragement for the commitment we need to make one to the other. Commitment embraces the other four star qualities.

And The Greatest Of These Is Love

The simple command to "love one another" should be enough said; however, the unconditional love or "agape" love is deeper than the ocean, higher than the highest mountain and encompasses every possible emotion within us. I saw a man on the six o'clock news with tears streaming down his face say, " I'm sorry for what my son has done, I don't understand why he did it, but I want him to know, I still love him." What his son had done was shoot a deputy in the head at point blank range. The father was loving unconditionally, not the action of his son, but his son.

Love not only encompasses every emotion but also leads to a life of integrity, respect, reliability, and commitment. It is the one true bond to star power in the five most important areas of our lives. In I John 3:18 "My little children (meaning children of God), let us not love in word or in tongue but in deed and in truth."

Love is so shallow if only spoken but so powerful if shown in deed and truth. True love allows us to be a star.

At the beginning of this chapter I mentioned that achieving star status took hard work, determination, and perseverance. Being recognized as a star means you're the best. So, how do you measure up? Here's a tool to help determine your star status at being the best son/daughter, brother/sister, husband/wife, father/mother and grandfather/grandmother you can be. On a scale of 1 to 10 with 10 being the highest, rate yourself and determine what areas you need to improve on to reach star status and be your best.

	Son Daughter	Brother Sister	Husband Wife	Father Mother	Grandfather Grandmother
Integrity					
Respect					
Reliability					
Commitment					
LOVE					

My challenge to you is that *"You Too Can Be A Star — In The Five Most Important Areas Of Your Life"* and by doing so the improvement in this world of mankind would be significant beyond comprehension. Be a star, be a star, and be a bright and shining star!

ABOUT
CHET R. MARSHALL

*C*het Marshall is an entrepreneur, author, consultant and speaker. He *has practical, hands-on experience in finance, public education, health care, industry and retail (as a franchiser and franchisee). He is a general partner for a venture capital partnership. He's traveled extensively around the world, and his work as a speaker has taken him to all 50 states and most of the provinces of Canada. Chet speaks on motivation, leadership and successfully dealing with life's challenges. He has conducted numerous seminars for the Medical Group Management Association. He is an active member of the National Speakers Association and the Fellowship of Christian Athletes.*

Contact Information:
Chet R. Marshall
130 Summit Ridge
Hurricane, WV 25526
Phone: (304) 757-1985
E-mail: ChetinWV@aol.com

PUTTING YOUR BEST FOOT AND FORK ON THE ROAD

by Betty Pichon

He placed the phone back in its cradle and just sat numb for a few seconds. Then wow! This was it. The CEO had just called him to invite him to dinner. This *had* to be it. This had to be the night he would be given the branch manager job in the newly opened London office. His heart was pounding; he couldn't wait to tell his friends. He was going to be an international manager. Chuck's feet didn't hit the floor for the rest of the day.

That night at dinner, he arrived at the restaurant way ahead of the CEO, George. While waiting for George to arrive, Chuck ordered a little pre-celebration drink. He had been so excited all day; he had not eaten lunch, but just had a few potato chips from the vending machine. The drink hit him right away but certainly put him in a festive mood. Just as Chuck finished the drink, George appeared. He was a tall graying man with distinguished features. He was dressed impeccably. Of course, he could afford to. He made the big bucks. Chuck was wearing his best suit as well but, unfortunately, had not been able to pick up his shirts from the laundry, so he was forced to wear the one with the spot on the front. But then his tie would cover the spot so why worry?

George ordered a wonderful bottle of wine. "Phew," thought Chuck, "I really don't need anything else, but how can I refuse?" As the meal progressed, Chuck got louder and louder. He slurred a few words, but he wasn't worried; he knew the right things to say. George watched with great interest as Chuck signaled the waiter with his napkin to order more water, crumbled crackers in his soup, wiped his knife on the table-cloth, and actually left the spoon in his coffee cup when he drank.

The dinner was over and Chuck was so excited. This must be when George would give him the good news that he had been chosen for the London job. But, strangely, George stood up, thanked Chuck for joining him for the evening and left.

It's no surprise why Chuck was not given the job. In today's com-petitive market, it's not enough to be the most skilled; you must know the proper etiquette for the occasion as well. Of course, there's nothing new about treating others with sensitivity and respect. The news is that corporate executives all over the world are seeking expert guidance on matters of etiquette. Whether employees are doing business on the tele-phone, by e-mail at lunch or just around the water cooler, they project an image that reflects the entire corporation. The wrong image can cost many, many dollars in lost business. In highly competitive markets where companies offer similar services at similar costs, how people behave may be as important to a company's success as the quality or price of its product. Think about the time you were not served with respect and courtesy. You probably did not go back to that place again unless you absolutely had no choice. Then, you probably told all your friends about how rudely you were treated.

It's the little things that count! Trite as this might sound, nowhere does it hold more truth and power than in the competitive world of business where the niceties and social amenities can mean the difference between simply existing and gaining the edge so necessary for success.

The world has changed considerably from the days when our grandmothers taught us how to act in social situations. Today we have become high tech and complicated. Yet basic courtesies have never gone out of style. Automation has become an integral part of our lives. Like it or not, innovations like voice mail, fax machines and electronic mail are here to stay. The more high tech our world becomes, the more important effective inter-personal communication will be.

Men and women have become colleagues. Each year women continue to be promoted to management positions but not without some kinks. Social rules from yesteryear are suddenly called into question. Men today are asking questions like, "Is it appropriate for me to initiate a handshake before a woman extends her hand?" "When introducing a female manager to a male customer, whose name should I say first?" Likewise women are asking, "When a man approaches me, should I stand? When taking a male client to lunch, how can I tactfully let the server know that I will be picking up the check?"

Yes, it's the little things that count. Business etiquette is not difficult, it means simply *knowing what to do and when to do it.*

Handshakes and greetings are usually the first contact we have with another person. The more comfortable we feel in this activity the better the tone for the whole meeting.

When do you shake hands? The rule is — all the time!

- When you run into someone you know
- When you say goodbye to the same person
- When someone comes in from the outside to see you in your office and when someone leaves
- When someone enters your home or when you enter someone else's home

- When you are congratulating someone — after a speech, or after an award presentation

When do you not shake hands?

- When the other person has his or her hands full

- When the other person you want to greet is someone much higher ranked than you and to whom you really have nothing to say. In this case, it would look pushy for you to rush up and shake hands and introduce yourself.

- When the other person is eating messy food in one hand and holding a drink in the other hand. Instead say, "I know you can't shake hands now, but hello."

There are just a few rules that you need to know.

- When you enter a group, shake hands first with your host and then with the other most senior person in the room. If everyone is clustered together — people of all ranks — don't worry about whose hand you shake next, as long as you have shaken the hand of the host.

- A handshake should be firm, not limp and fishlike. Grasp the hand of the other person high on the hand, the web between your thumb and forefinger fitting into the web of the other person's hand. Just a few shakes, then release. Do not try to break bones!

- If someone doesn't see your hand extended and doesn't offer his or her hand to you, just draw back your hand and smile. That person is not rejecting you on purpose; he or she simply doesn't see your extended hand. It's an embarrassing two or three seconds for you, but it happens to everyone who shakes hands often.

- Men, do not wait for a woman to extend her hand — offer yours right away.
- Women, always stand, just as men do, when shaking the hand of someone who has just entered the room.

Introductions

The protocol of making proper introductions is very logical. You simply introduce a less to a more important or senior person. For example:

- Always introduce a younger person to an older person
- A junior executive to a senior executive
- A fellow executive to a customer or client
- An unofficial person to an official person
- A fellow U.S. citizen to a peer from another country

Sometimes introductions can be hazardous, but you can breeze through them with just a little knowledge of what to do and when to do it. For example, explain who people are when you introduce them. Such as, "Barbara, I'd like to introduce Ben James, my uncle. Ben, this is Senator Barbara Brown, the chair of the appropriations committee." If you are introducing someone with a title, such as senator, governor, general or mayor, always be sure to give the person's last name and the state he or she is from.

Remember to use titles when introducing people. You may know someone as James Howard, but when you are introducing him, it's important to give his title, such as Judge James Howard. Some titles accompany their owner to their graves. Once an ambassador, always an ambassador. When a general retires he is still addressed as "General." The same is true for governor, senator, judge or president.

It's the little things that count. Our image is a part of our credibility. This goes beyond the purely visual aspects of fashion, dress for success, and the proper colors for skin tones. Image involves our self-conduct and personal standards.

We are all walking billboards. What people see is what they believe. People respond to you according to what you show them. Uniforms prove this. If we see someone in a police uniform, we automatically think that person is a member of the police force. If we see a man in priest's clothing, we believe he is a man of God. If you walked into a boardroom and saw a woman dressed in a mini-skirt, fishnet stockings, spike heels, and a feather boa, would you believe she was a serious businesswoman? Well, probably, but not the business you were there for.

Herb Kelleher, Southwest Airlines chairman, is a master of understanding the nuance of any situation. When Herb is with his employees, he is dressed as they are. He joins in with the flight attendants and serves passengers. He sometimes wears a chicken suit when flying to make it more fun. Southwest calls its mode of dress for its employees funwear. By wearing 'fun clothing' they feel much freer and can be playful with the passengers. It gives the passengers permission to relax and have fun as well. But, notice the pilots, the people who hold our lives in their hands. They always wear the typical pilot's uniform. Can you imagine your pilot coming on the plane dressed in cutoffs and sandals? I'd be willing to bet there would be a stampede to get off that aircraft. Southwest has mastered the nuances of the flying profession. Herb Kelleher may be in a chicken suit entertaining passengers, but when he is in a union negotiation or addressing an audience, you can bet he is dressed in the best business manner.

What does your billboard say about you? Do you think about what you are advertising everyday when you get dressed? Are you conveying the message you want to your client, boss or friend? Each situation has a different billboard advertisement. The days of the skirted suit or three-piece suit have changed dramatically over the years. In many cases, to wear these would be inappropriate.

Casual Fridays have now evolved in many businesses into casual weeks. But most companies have found that if they did not specify just exactly what casual was, employees showed up in everything from cutoffs to well-pressed chinos. It is almost impossible to have a dress code that spells out every little detail. That would tend to be very restrictive. It is up to the employee to know what the proper attire is for the business and for his or her own career. The best rule of thumb is to remember who you are, what you want to project, and what you want to achieve.

Studies have shown that employees behave the way they are dressed. Even if they do not see the customer or client in person, their demeanor is determined by the way they are dressed. If an employee is dressed in cutoff jeans and T-shirt, the manner in which he or she deals with a customer on the phone is much more relaxed and in some cases flippant. When dressed in a more professional manner, the employee is more likely to treat the customer with respect and in a businesslike manner.

The image we project at mealtime is just as important as any other time. Remember the story of Chuck and how he damaged his chances for a promotion by using poor table manners. Really polished table manners can take you to another level of sophistication. Obviously, everyone will notice (in a negative way) if you eat with your mouth open or use your flatware ineptly, but you can also really impress top executives if you know the fine points of dining — how to eat an artichoke, for example, or snails. With these finer skills in hand, you become even more valuable as a representative of your company and even more sought after as a dinner guest.

Fortunately, while some other aspects of good manners are linked to personal qualities such as tact and the ability to get along with others, table manners can belong to anyone. No one is born with them, and once you have acquired a usable set, using them becomes second nature. Once you have mastered the essentials of eating properly, it is fine to be casual about them. Many of the strict and unnecessary rules of even a decade ago have vanished. For example, it is not particularly important to follow the old rule about opening a dinner size napkin halfway and a luncheon napkin all the way. Remembering to put the napkin in your lap is the important thing. I am not going to give you a seminar on table etiquette, but just a few dos and don'ts that will help when you are in the same position as Chuck.

- Never put your napkin on your lap until everyone is seated.
- Remember your liquids (coffee, water, wine) will be on your right and your solids (bread, salad) on the left.
- Do not hold the soup spoon with the handle in the palm of your hand. Hold it with the thumb across the top of the handle.
- Always spoon the soup away from you rather than toward you.
- Never, never, never, crumble crackers in your soup.
- Always tear a bite size piece of your roll; butter, and then eat. Do not butter the whole roll or put the whole roll in your mouth.
- Don't chew with your mouth open.
- Don't dunk. Anything!
- If you leave your chair for a moment, put your napkin on your chair.

- Always ask someone to pass you whatever it is you want. Do not do the boardinghouse reach.
- If you do not want coffee, wine, tea, etc. just put two fingers on the bowl of the vessel when the waiter is ready to pour. This signals "I don't want any, thank you." Never turn your glass or cup upside down.
- If you are served a beverage and do not want it, just don't drink it!
- Don't mash all your food together in the center of your plate.
- When finished with the meal, leave your knife and fork on the plate in the ten minutes to four position.
- Don't stack your dishes in front of you. Wait for the server to remove them.

Bon appetit.

The Language of Leadership

In communications:

Most people think that some of us are born with the 'gift of gab' and some of us aren't. But the truth is that there is no 'gift of gab.' People who are good at conversation just know a few simple skills that anyone can learn.

As you grew up, adults taught you how to read, write, add, and subtract. As you made mistakes, they corrected you until you mastered these skills. Conversational skills are another matter. You were taught to pronounce words, but perhaps nobody ever taught you how to improve or even told that you needed improvement. People either did not warm up to you, or they went away and looked for someone else who could converse with them.

When you started your career, you found that the supervisors, managers and your peers corrected you when you used the wrong words for the business. In your social life, it was your date that would correct you on the proper way to converse. Now after all that, you'd think you'd know all there is to know about communication, wouldn't you. Well, not so. Somehow we forget or just do not keep up with all the changes that go on everyday.

In communicating a spoken message, it is interesting to note that 55 percent of what you project is the body language you use, 38 percent is the tone of voice you use, and only 7 percent is the word choices you use.

Today's society is full of cliches and jargon, most of which does not produce a very intelligent portrayal of the speaker. People are "sick of slick" talk. They want to be communicated with in simple, understandable language.

People are strongly influenced by what they see more than what they hear. So start your conversations in an open body position. Let your arms rest naturally at your sides (relaxed, not "at attention"). What you will find is that, almost immediately, your hands will begin to gesture easily. The moment you put you hands in your pockets (and heaven forbid) jiggle your change, or clasp your hands in front of you, you begin to look nervous and you restrict your ability to gesture naturally. When your hands are at your sides and gesturing openly, you will communicate a relaxed confidence.

Always maintain eye contact. This makes you appear more credible, more relaxed, and more interesting. It also forces the other person to look back at you. Remember to smile. A smile is especially appropriate when introducing yourself, but at all other times as well. A smile communicates confidence and sincerity. When it isn't appropriate to smile, you can use your eyes and eyebrows to communicate. Raised eyebrows are the classic facial gesture of commitment and caring. Use all of your face expressively to support your words.

Many women and some men have a tendency to end their sentences with an upward tone of voice. This sounds as if you are asking a question, even when you are stating a very serious point. Keep the sentence endings on the same voice level as the rest of the sentence unless you are asking a question. The lower your voice is, the more credible it sounds, Start by tape recording yourself talking. If you hear your voice going up at the ends of sentences, repeat them, forcing your intonation lower.

If a man nods his head to show agreement and a woman nods her head to show she's listening, this may lead a man to assume she is agreeing with him, when, in reality, the woman is just paying attention to what he has to say. Many times you will be nodding without knowing it, so if you do not agree with a person, you have to make sure you say so verbally. In this way there will be no misunderstanding on either side.

Remember, tonality is most important to getting your points across. If you speak in a monotone, people will lose their concentration and their minds will go elsewhere. A high-pitched voice will grate on your listeners. Try to lower the tone of your voice. You can do it. Practice at various levels until you find one that feels right for you, and then work at making the lower pitch your normal tone. There are many books that will help you with this exercise, and a tape recorder is an absolute must. Using the language of leadership is one of the most important aspects of a career. It is a part of your billboard message. If your billboard says you are well-dressed and groomed appropriately for the situation and then your voice comes out totally opposite, you have lost your listeners. They will be confused by the mixed message they are receiving.

If you decided to read this chapter, you probably are already savvy on the subject. It has been my purpose to perhaps remind you of a few tips that can be overlooked in our daily lives. Etiquette rules change often. We are all still learning. This is truly a global society and with it comes a need for more uniform ways of dealing with people. I hope you have picked up some additional tips and suggestions for helping you move more quickly toward your wholehearted success.

ABOUT
BETTY PICHON

*B*etty *Pichon is the Founder of The Pichon Group, an Executive Development firm based in Phoenix, Arizona. She conducts comprehensive coaching, training and consulting. Ms. Pichon advises and instructs corporate executives and others to master their marketing, customer retention and public speaking skills, as well as how to polish their professionalism. She masterfully promotes greater awareness and self-confidence in today's competitive economy by sharpening personal skills that put a person in control of any business or social situation.*

Ms. Pichon is a graduate of the most prestigious protocol and etiquette school in the world, The At-Ease-Corporation, headquartered in Cincinnati with offices in New York and London. She received her B.A. degree from the University of Arizona and an M.BA. from Emory University.

Contact Information:
Betty Pichon
6821 E. Thunderbird Road
Scottsdale, AZ 85254
Phone: (480) 596-7997
Fax: (480) 596-5237
E-mail: BPichon956@aol.com

USING ASSERTIVE COMMUNICATION TECHNIQUES TO DEAL WITH DIFFICULT PEOPLE

by Marsha Petrie Sue, M.B.A.

Have you ever tried to change another human being? I have — only to conclude it makes for great first marriages. The basis of encouraging cooperation begins with our own behavior. We cannot control, change, or mold people into more cooperative beings.

For wholehearted success we should take an inward look to determine where we stand on the assertiveness scale. What is your typical approach? Passive, aggressive or assertive?

Passive: Compliant. Passive behavior is that behavior which allows others to violate your rights. You become a doormat and let people walk all over you. Typically, the passive person loses and everyone else wins. Their behavioral goals are to be liked, to be nice. Overriding this behavior is the desire to avoid conflict at all cost. Total cooperation is the name of the game. Their message can be very frustrating: "What I think doesn't matter. What I feel is unimportant. I don't respect myself and I don't expect you to either. Everyone has rights but me. Nice people don't disagree. Peace at any price."

Aggressive: Ready! Fire! Aim! is their motto. Aggressive behavior allows you to stand up for your rights while violating the rights of others. Aggressive people are bullies, ego-centered, and full of themselves. Their behavioral goals are typically to win, boss others around, frighten, conquer, and win at all cost! To get what they want, when they want it! Their message of "You will never have to wonder what I think or how I feel — I am going to tell you! You are even more stupid than I thought, if you disagree! I'm OK — you're not. People should do what I want without questioning me or they will pay dearly. If more people were like me, we wouldn't have the problems we have. I don't need to listen to anybody. They have nothing to offer me."

Assertive: To declare positively. Assertive behavior is behavior that allows you to stand up for your rights while valuing the rights of others. You can say no without feeling guilty and without losing your job. You have great respect for yourself and at the same time, a great respect for others. You create a win for you and a win for others. The behavioral goals of assertive people are generally to get the work done at a level of excellence while enhancing the growth and development of those doing the work. They communicate in a style that is accurate and respectful of the dignity of all people involved. You will hear them say, "I have no interest in being critical of you for what you think, want, need, or feel. I encourage sharing these ideas with me. We are here to get the job done and to contribute to a positive work environment."

The assertive person's key thoughts are, "We all have rights that are equal. Let me know what I can improve because I want to learn from my mistakes. I have choices, and I am responsible for the consequences of my decisions. I am not a helpless victim and I will not allow others to decide for me how I will behave. Conflicts provide opportunities to grow and are not something to be avoided. They can lead to a higher level of cooperation."

"For good or ill, your conversation is your advertisement.
Every time you open your mouth
you let others look into your mind." – Bruce Barton

Think of passive, assertive, and aggressive as points of a continuum. Where do you fit?

1 2 3 4 5 6 7 8 9 10 9 8 7 6 5 4 3 2 1
Passive   **Assertive**   **Aggressive**

The assertive communicator understands the choices available when cooperation is the desired end result in dealing with challenging people:

1. Stay and do nothing. This may not mean we wimp out and fold. This decision may be based on the importance of the situation. Is it worth the time and energy? Is the issue so important that battling with the other person is critical to a better outcome? A key learning I have experienced is to pick your battles. Otherwise you live your life in conflict and turmoil, allowing every encounter to become a confrontation. Your stress level remains high while your success remains low, and you are pushed into either the passive or aggressive mode.

2. Leave. Maybe a better way to say this is take a time out. An assertive person will reject the situation as it stands right now. If you want to lead the communication to cooperation, the other person may be too enraged to do so. My husband and I have a deal. If one of us gets really upset, the other partner can call a time out — or even the enraged person can do this. The completion to this rule is for the person that called the time out to come back within 24 hours to resolve the situation, not to just kick it under the rug.

3. Change your Attitude. Assertive people realize this as an option. I have studied the effects of attitude on the outcomes we get — especially when cooperation is the goal. We are dominated by negativism. This is one reason I will not listen to the news in the morning. It can taint my entire day. Studies show the average person talks to themselves approximately 77 percent of the time with negative self-talk. And to exacerbate this, we talk approximately 600 to 800 words per minute in our heads. We are always analyzing everything and giving events a pessimistic view.

I have learned to use the freeze frame to change this negative self-talk to positive. Each thought we have filters through a past frame of reference. An event, something someone said, a memorable encounter, and much more become the frames of reference we pass our thoughts through. When I catch myself saying something negative, I will consciously react, freeing that frame of reference and changing it into a more positive thought, hence the freeze frame. This process does take considerable focus and willingness to change in order to move from the negative to the positive. When we take this risk, we change our attitude and, therefore, are able to stand up for our rights while not violating the rights of others.

4. Change your Behavior. In studying behavioral psychology I have learned that it is often easier to change your attitude first, and your behavior will follow. If I consciously change my thinking to be more optimistic, my behavior and actions automatically follow. The idea of tricking myself into an optimistic outlook is appealing because we do become a self-fulfilling prophecy with regards to our behavior. As Henry Ford said, "Whether you can or can't, you're absolutely right." If you believe you will succeed, you will. If you believe you can think more positively, you will. Belief in yourself is driven by the desire to be different tomorrow than you are today and by the attitude that you can change and succeed.

*"I do what I say, I say what I think,
I think what I feel."* — Mahatma Gandhi

Mary Lee Tracy, from the Cincinnati Gymnastics Academy and coach to many Olympic greats says, "The mind could be what makes or breaks someone. It's the strongest muscle in your body that really controls everything else. When that baby's weak, you're in trouble." We need to train our brain to develop that muscle, inputting the smart techniques to encourage cooperation.

1. Bull's eye or sitting duck? We must know what our target is in order to establish cooperation. What do we want the person to say or do differently? What do we want the outcome to be? Developing a specific target will drive the process to success. Understanding the specific actions we must employ will ensure hitting the bull's eye. If we don't have a direction, the chances of our winding up someplace we don't want to be is predestined! We become a sitting duck. The situation will quickly elevate to dissension and anger. Dr. Stephen Covey says to begin with the end in mind which is one of his *Seven Habits of Highly Effective People*. Focus on what you want rather than on what you don't want. If we understand what the target is and maintain focus on what we want, our muscle power in our brain will drive the actions to achieve that success subconsciously. When we approach a situation where cooperation is the desired goal, we must concentrate on the Bull's eye or we do become a sitting duck!

2. Massage your message. The mirroring technique in communication is how we massage our message so the receiver understands our goal. Two points to consider are mirroring and communication style. When we want someone to cooperate and they are standing, we need to stand up, too. If they sit, sit along beside them. Mirror, don't mimic, their body language. Remember the natural barriers, like a table or desk.

These become boundaries and need to be eliminated in most cases. Also awareness of the other person's communication style is essential. Are they slower paced? We must slow our gestures and rate of speech to match theirs. They may be faster paced. We must pick up the rate of speech to be similar to theirs. Simply put, people like people who are like themselves. So we need to match their style, not to parrot or mimic them, but to adhere to the Dr. Tony Alessandra's Platinum Rule: Do unto others as they want to be done unto!

Four communication styles to consider are:

Relaters: Mostly slower paced, they love people, are tremendously loyal, and building a relationship is critical. We find these people choosing teaching, social work, and healthcare as their typical fields of endeavor.

Logical thinkers: These people are normally slower paced, analytical, detail oriented, data loving, and task oriented. They can seem aloof and distant. Logicals are likely to be engineers, accountants, statisticians, and other detail oriented disciplines.

Socializers: faster paced, people oriented, verbal, and fun loving. They love to be rewarded and, at times, are not focused. Public relations, sales, and marketing become their fields of choice.

Directors: faster paced. They like power and control, are focused and task oriented, and need the bottom line. These people love to be in a leadership role, and we see them as team leaders, supervisors, managers, and CEOs.

Much research has been conducted on these four styles of communications. Smart techniques to establish cooperation includes being able to flex to their style because the chance of our changing them is nil. We can only change ourselves — though we continue to try to change others! We don't have to become them, just be aware of what they are so we can mirror elements of their style rather than our own intrinsic style.

Easier said than done, especially under stress!

3. Flex your mind muscle. Agree to disagree. I've learned we don't always have to be right. Learn to choose your battles. Some people continue to walk this earth looking for a fight. Medical studies from many of the leading universities continue to tell us this mind set takes a toll on our health. The constant high levels of adrenaline and cortisol, both stress hormones, will tear down our immune system to the point of making us very ill and eventually killing us. In my opinion, life's too short and there is too much to enjoy to let anger get the best of me!

4. Involve to resolve. Amicably, you both agree and are willing to work on the solution together to achieve the results you want. You see the benefit and so does the other person. This means every part of our communication is focused on a positive outcome, a specific flexible plan is in place, and we are willing to share this optimistically. We must

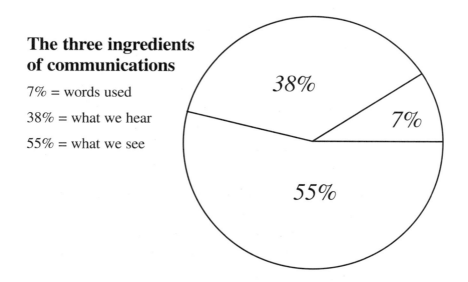

The three ingredients of communications

7% = words used

38% = what we hear

55% = what we see

focus on congruency in every element of communications. Our listening must be sincere, our words heartfelt, and our body language open.

"All bitter feelings are avoided, or at least greatly reduced by prompt, face-to-face discussion." — Walter B. Pitkin

When our communication degenerates from our goal of cooperation, we must observe where the other person falls on our most unwanted list. This list identifies the seven most difficult people to create cooperation with and how to handle them better. Learning these traits allows us to train our brain and flex our communication muscle.

1. The Dominating Tyrant
2. The Back Stabber
3. The Clam
4. The Opinionated Expert
5. The Needy Agonizer
6. The Fault Finder
7. The Whine and Cheeser

1. The Dominating Tyrant. They stay in control by putting others down and are typically quick to discount ideas or changes they did not initiate. If their ideas are countered, their buttons are pushed and they will move even further from cooperation. Sometimes they are unwilling to entertain thoughts conflicting with their ideas.

Their message usually includes:
- "Let me have my own way or I'll embarrass or humiliate you."
- "Defer decisions to me and I will pretend I like you and you won't be criticized."

Our internal message includes:
- *"Why is he mad at me?"*
- *"Why does she dislike me so much to say such things?"*

- *"He can't talk to me that way. I'll show him!"*

In handling the Dominating Tyrant we want to be assertive — to stand up for our rights while not violating the rights of others. Recognize how self-involved and ego-oriented they are, and try not to throw disagreements in their face. We will rarely win! An assertive person will say:

- "Kim, as I was saying, I have a solution for this problem."
- "It seems we've reached a stalemate here. Let me think over your ideas."
- "That is very true and that is definitely a first step. I'd like your ideas on additional steps."

Behaviors to avoid with the Dominating Tyrant:

- Do not take their explosions personally.
- Do not put yourself down. That's what they want you to do!
- Do not avoid them.

2. The Back Stabber. These people are easily identifiable because they typically attack from behind your back — not directly. They will stab you with putdowns, criticism, and false rumors, pretending they have done nothing.

The message they send:

- "Don't mess with me or I'll get you from behind later, and be careful what you say about me or I'll say something that will embarrass you in front of others."
- "There is nothing you can do to stop me. I am more clever than you."

Our internal message includes:

- *"Maybe she is right. Maybe I'm not doing as well as I should be."*
- *"Who keeps saying these terrible things about me?"*
- *"Does everyone else think the same thing?"*

To handle the Back Stabber: An assertive person will catch him or her in the act, call the behavior, and be ready for denials. Don't create a fight. Don't directly challenge Back Stabbers in public. Just let them know you caught them, allow them a way to save face, and confront them in private.

- "That did sound like you were serious. Do the rest of you feel that way? Is this becoming a problem?"
- "Dan, I heard some people mentioning that you're unhappy with the plan I implemented. You know how important I think feedback is. I wanted to take some time to hear what you really think. I value your opinions."

Behaviors to avoid with the Back Stabber:
- They will probably get worse rather than better, so don't wait for them to change.
- Never underestimate their power for destruction and the damage they can do.
- Do not laugh. Let them know you heard the cutting remark and take it seriously.

3. The Clam. Our next person won't talk or offer information when you try to hold a discussion. This person will escape involvement by saying "I don't know" and similar phrases and will answer questions with a yes, no, or grunt.

The message they send:
- "Leave me alone and you won't have to deal with my silence."
- "Don't confront me because it won't do you any good."
- "Be careful. I might blow up and become passive-aggressive if you push too hard."

Our internal message includes:
- *"Why are they so upset with me?"*
- *"This silence is unbearable. Are they doing this on purpose?"*

- *"What can I say to get them to open up?"*

An assertive person understands the need to ask the Clam open-ended questions. Pay particular attention and use open body language that demonstrates you are listening. Don't jump in and relieve the pressure. Instead, try counting to 30. Discuss what keeps them from talking. The language we direct to the Clam is focused and process oriented.

- "It seems like you're giving this some thought. What's coming to mind?"
- "That is very true and that is definitely a first step. I'd like your ideas on additional steps."

Behaviors to avoid with the Clam:

- Do not let the Clam think he or she is getting away with silence.
- Do not criticize the Clam for not talking or for allowing too much silence.

4. The Opinionated Expert will present opinions as if he or she knows everything about a subject. This person will use a condescending tone and act as if there is always something extraordinary about what he or she knows. The Opinionated Expert likes to leave very little room for differences in opinion and will find someone else or something else to blame if a decision backfires.

The message they send:

- "Don't bother to argue with me because I will always have a way to find something wrong with your ideas."
- "Disagree with me in public and you'll find yourself put down and made to look stupid."
- "My mind is set in stone so don't bother to persuade me."

Our internal message includes:

- *"She knows so much. I won't bother to mention my idea."*

- *"Maybe I don't know what I'm talking about."*
- *"It's no use. I can't get anywhere with her."*

The assertive communicator knows to prepare before disagreeing with the Opinionated Expert. Conversation should include paraphrasing ideas so the other person's ego will be protected. Another technique is to position counterpoints in the form of questions and present alternatives as related ideas.

Include giving credit, if appropriate, when responding to the Opinionated Expert.

- "If I heard you correctly, the major points are . . ."
- "You're the expert in this case and you may be right. Help me understand . . ."
- "If we take your idea and implement it, what problems do you see arising in the first six months?"

Behaviors to avoid:

- Do not try to be a counter expert. You will only make the Opinionated Expert more critical.
- Do not put yourself down.
- Do not try to embarrass the expert. He or she will usually be prepared to do the same.

5. Needy Agonizers will commit themselves when faced with difficult decisions and will tend to be very agreeable — everything sounds good, yet they still will not make a decision. This is perpetuated by a strong need to be liked and approved.

The message they send:

- "I am nice to you, so you owe it to me to be nice back, but when I say 'yes' I mean maybe."
- "I'll do what I can to get you to like me, and you should feel guilty if you do anything that is less than supportive of me."

- "Don't ask me what I want or like; I'm not sure anymore."

Our internal message includes

- *"Do I come on so strong that she's afraid to disagree?"*
- *"Why won't he just speak up if he disagrees?"*
- *"I guess I should force myself to be nice. She's nice!"*

The assertive person will make it easy for the Needy Agonizer to disagree by helping to identify priorities by using the decision process. The agonizer may have concerns and issues that are being kept private so we must make honesty safe. Once the agonizer has made a decision, support him or her with encouragement and optimism.

- "I'm glad you basically agree with my proposal. Every proposal has its weak points. What parts could be improved? Tell me the good and the bad."
- "Let's make a wish list of pros and cons to help clarify this."
- "It seems that you've identified a number of advantages. Can you help me rank order them?"

Behaviors to avoid:

- Do not allow agonizing over small decisions.
- Do not fail to follow up. Go out of your way a few times to make an agonizer feel good about decisions.

6. The Fault Finder tends to criticize everything. This person uses a tone of voice implying someone else is always at fault. The Fault Finder sees nothing wrong with complaining to you about one person and then later complaining to that same person about you.

The message:

- "I'm right once in a while, so you had better be sure and listen to me."
- "Don't expect me to do anything to fix problems; I'm helpless."

- "I am perfect. Therefore, it is my duty to notice all of these faults around me."

Our internal message includes:

- *"Maybe this office is full of problems."*
- *"Why won't he just speak up if he disagrees?"*
- *"Should I be noticing more of these problems?"*

An assertive person knows the best way to handle a Fault Finder is to redirect the conversation with statements setting time limits or goals. Minimize complaining by paying attention to important ideas and overlooking criticism. Always confront this person privately, especially when the criticism is destroying a relationship.

- "Can I ask you another question before I get back to my project? What . . ."
- "From what I've seen, I don't think that's true. Whenever I've gone to them with a problem, they've been open and helpful."

Behaviors to avoid:

- Do not allow yourself to agree for the sake of silencing the criticism.
- Do not reinforce complaints by politely listening and remaining silent.
- Do not let him or her get away without taking any responsibility for solutions.

7. The Whine and Cheeser characteristics include taking the approach that life consists of "just getting by" and "doing the best that you can against the odds." This person thinks life will continue to get even worse and can come up with endless lists of why something won't work. We will rarely be able to convince this person of much, so we won't spend much time here! Their message is:

- "Give up your dreaming and optimistic thinking".

- "You'd better discuss your ideas with me, you may miss seeing the mistakes you are bound to make."

The best approach with a Whine and Cheeser is to let what is said go in one ear and out the other. Almost impossible to argue with as this person's extreme negativism keeps him or her from being reasonable or hearing rational, positive solutions. So what can we do?

- Learn to restate your case for the record and for your own mental health.
- Think of the worst thing that could happen and work backwards.

"If I really want to improve my situation,
I can work on the thing over which I have control – myself."
— Stephen R. Covey

What will you do now to apply these smart techniques to encourage success?

1. Identify the needs and benefits for both.
2. Change the pattern of interaction.
3. Agree where disagreements can coexist.

Homework and Next Steps

The style of my difficult person is _____.

My goal and target is to _____.

The actual words I will use are: "_____."

I will address this issue by (deadline to apply these techniques):_____.

"If it's meant to be, it's up to me!"

ABOUT
MARSHA PETRIE SUE, M.B.A.

arsha Petrie Sue, M.B.A. is living her life's mission, to give back more than she's received and to connect her head and heart with her mouth. She has had a blessed life and infuses clients with motivation and energy to live their life's dreams. Marsha has 25+ years in sales and executive management and she is the CEO of Communicating Results, Inc., a speaking and training organization. Her company provides customized keynotes and workshops for employees and executives who want to improve communications, customer service and personal acceptance to change by building morale and individual motivation.

She is an author, speaker, coach and workshop leader traveling throughout the United States and overseas. Her clients include The Doctors' Company, Association of Legal Administrators, Enterprise Rent-a-Car, Bacon and Dear law corporation, Mortgage Bankers Association of America, and the Pampered Chef. Participants in Marsha's seminars frequently comment on her energy, humor, charisma, professional delivery and depth of knowledge. Besides feeling motivated, Marsha leaves the audiences with practical advice and methods to succeed. She holds a B.A. from California State University and an M.B.A. from the University of Phoenix.

Contact Information:
Marsha Petrie Sue, M.B.A.
Communicating Results, Inc.
P.O. Box 15218
Scottsdale, AZ 85267
Phone: (480) 661-8756
Fax: (480) 661-8755
E-mail: Marsha@CommunicatingResults.com
Website: www.MarshaPetrieSue.com

SOLVING EMPLOYEE PROBLEMS

by Michael E. Rega

You manage a machine shop in the Northeast. Your machine shop is just one part of a factory that produces aftermarket parts for the auto industry. There are several department heads in the building like you overseeing different stages of the manufacturing process. One day, at about three o'clock, your best worker, Joe, enters your glass cubicle and says, "Boss, I'll be leaving now." You glance at your watch and reply, "OK Joe, if you need some time this afternoon, sure. See you tomorrow." Now you have a personal stake in giving Joe flexibility. This guy is amazing. If you tell Joe today that you need a part completed yesterday, he almost makes the deadline! Catching you completely off guard Joe says, "No boss, I mean I'll be leaving now, for good." You catapult out of your seat and protest, "Joe, Joe, why don't you sit down for a moment and let's talk. Are you unhappy with the job? I can move you to a new project."

"No boss, I'm not unhappy."

You try again. " Do you need more time off?"

"No boss, I feel good."

Your guesses go nowhere until you finally ask, "Joe, what's up?"

He replies, "Boss, Mrs. Joe has decided that she wants to go back to work after all these years, and since we have only one car, I have to quit."

"Wait, wait Joe, please . . . what kind of job is she looking for?"

"Anything boss."

You have an interesting problem that may have several solutions. Let us consider some of the top potential solutions to Joe's and your problem.

1. Find another way for Joe to get to work: public transportation, carpool, bicycle.
2. Find another person to do Joe's job.
3. Find a job for Mrs. Joe.

After forty seconds or so of careful consideration, which is perhaps thirty seconds longer than some companies would take, you decide to tell Joe to sit tight for a moment, and you go to another department. The pieces-to-pieces department has a rather simple task. The employees take plastic parts from one box, stamp them onto another part and toss them into another box. With routine work like this, it is difficult to keep good employees, and turnover in this department is a huge issue. You confidently walk into the manager's office to ask a favor. "Tom, I have an employee issue that I need some help with. In a few days, a Mrs. Joe is going to come in looking for a job. If she can fog a mirror in the interview, hire her!" Two days later Mrs. Joe shows up, and, after adjusting the mirror several times, she fogs and is hired on the line. You are happy, Joe is back at work, and Tom has a new employee who has shown up for work two days in a row and all seems well. Then one day as Tom is sitting behind his pressboard, faux oak desk, he hears the most awful screams and shouts. He jumps to his feet sure that one of his employees has just accidentally removed a finger. As he runs outside, he discovers Mrs. Joe on the floor rolling around in an all-out hair pulling, scratching fight with Maria, his best employee.

Now, problem-solver, what is Tom to do?

1. Allow Mrs. Joe to beat up his best employee.

2. Break up the fight and fire Mrs. Joe.

3. Punt.

Tom breaks up the fight and separates Maria and Mrs. Joe. He emerges from the brawl with only minor scratches about his head and face and takes Maria to his office. He sits Maria down and asks, "OK, Maria, what's up?" to which Maria answers, " I have no idea, Tom. One minute I'm working and the next I'm being attacked from behind and pulled to the floor. The next thing I know, you are tearing the two of us apart." Tom gets nowhere.

Again, corporate problem-solver, what do you do?

1. Fire Mrs. Joe.

2. Fire Maria.

3. Speak with Mrs. Joe.

This story goes on and on and in so many corporate case studies of employee problems we, the management team, toil endlessly, stabbing into the darkness of problems without really knowing what we are doing.

Employee problems are usually a myriad of nested issues, so one of the first concepts to learn is that problems come nested. They are never delivered in neat little packages waiting for you to solve and move on.

In Phase 1 of Problem Solving the steps to follow are:

1. Separate the nested problems.

    a) Joe's transportation problem

    b) Mrs. Joe's unemployment

    c) Mrs. Joe's and Maria's fight

2. Prioritize the severity and immediacy of the problem. (In other words, as Mrs. Joe is nearly killing Maria, you should not be considering possible transportation for Joe.)

    a) Stop the fight.

      b) Joe's transportation

      c) Mrs. Joe's unemployment

3. Find the original cause. Before you adopt any solutions you must stop and discover the original cause. Every problem on our planet could be solved if we could get to and solve the original cause. Unfortunately, if you think for a second, what we actually do is treat symptoms.

      What causes cancer? You might say pollution, diet, sunlight, etc. All are correct. Take away the cause and you solve cancer. Yet, how do we typically fight cancer? Radiation, drugs, and surgery. This is obviously not a comprehensive treatment of the subject but meant as a model for problem solving.

Let us go back to Tom's situation where he has finally coaxed the writhing Mrs. Joe into his office. "Mrs. Joe, what just happened with Maria out there?" Mrs. Joe replies, "Boss, you know what's going on between Maria and my beloved Joe and I won't stand for it. In fact, if I get my hands on her again I'll pull her hair out." Whew! Tom has discovered the original cause.

In Phase 2 of Problem Solving (Assuming that you have discovered the original cause):

1. Assemble treatments — Do not discard any ideas until you have really considered their merit. A short list of treatments in this case could be:

      a) fire Joe and Mrs. Joe

      b) fire Maria

      c) provide company counseling for the Joes

      d) keep Mrs. Joe heavily sedated

      e) transfer Mrs. Joe back to Joe's manager.

2. Consider the consequences of each treatment.

If you fire Mrs. Joe and Joe, you may be making Maria happy, but now the machine shop would lose its best employee, and there are certainly going to be repercussions. You continue through the list of treatments and make a conscious decision for the best solution, knowing you are treating the causes and not the symptoms.

This process is quite different from the "just try it" attitude that most companies have toward problem solving. This single managerial style, if mastered, will propel your career to places you cannot yet imagine. It takes clarity of thought, sound unemotional judgement, and practice. However, once mastered, it is magical in its effectiveness.

Try it the next time the cubicle across the aisle rocks with conflict; after all, it is an opportunity to showcase your newest skill.

ABOUT
MICHAEL E. REGA

A popular speaker, author and instructor, Michael Rega entertains and educates thousands of people in professional organizations and in corporate America. He is also an executive Vice President with the Ecliptic Consulting Group, Inc./Persuasive Communication, ECG/PC, founded at Northwestern University in 1957 and a leader in adult development. Mike is frequently published in sales and training magazines including Training, The American Salesman, *and in industry insider newsletters, such as* The Imager.

Mike is an active member of the American Society for Training and Development and the National Speakers Association and is one of the original members of the International Association of Professional Negotiators. A graduate of Arizona State University, his graduate studies include engineering at Purdue University and foreign language and culture at the University of Iowa.

Contact Information:
Michael E. Rega
Ecliptic Consulting Group, Inc./
Persuasive Communication
P.O. Box 23807
Tempe, AZ 85285
Phone (800) 236-2980
Fax: (480) 899-3015
E-mail: AZEcliptic@aol.com
Website: www.ecgpc.com

EXECUTIVE COACHING – SUPERIOR PERFORMER'S SECRET WEAPON FOR SUCCESS

by Natalie Manor

"The 27 percent increase in profitability that our division produced is beyond anything I thought was possible when we first starting working together six months ago," said a very delighted Mark.

Mark is a happy man today. He reduced his number of working hours from an average of 70 hours per week to 55. He is spending more time with his executive team developing them rather than avoiding their hourly interruptions in his day; he has lost 14 pounds and just received a promotion to Executive VP — a promotion that he has longed for for six years. And in most part he owes all of this to his commitment to working with an executive coach eight months earlier.

In the last five years, coaching, especially executive coaching, has become commonplace in corporate America. And with good reason. Coaching can dramatically change the quality of one's life by creating clarity of purpose for the person involved in coaching. That person helps to create a workplace where superior performers want to work and thrive.

Most people want to know what the difference between coaching and consulting is — and how coaching appears to produce such dramatically improved results in a short period of time over the traditional consulting model.

The growing popularity of coaching has led to the need for a distinction between coaching and consulting. A clear explanation of coaching will also provide insight into how coaching produces dramatic results, despite the short period of time a client is assisted when compared to the traditional method of consulting.

A coach is hired to support an individual who seeks to find his or her purpose and build high-value relationships, both personal and within the organization. A very simple difference between coaching and consulting is that a consultant is hired to do the work, which may lead to a less interactive experience. In coaching, because the coach plays a support role, working as a guide rather than the leader, the client becomes more involved and therefore more proactive.

My clients have created dramatic results in very short periods of time because they define the playing field, decide the strategy, and measure the outcomes based upon their purpose, vision, and identity.

Imagine what it would be like if your workday was based on your highest purpose, your values and your outcomes were in alignment with your organization and your co-workers. It is not only possible to create such a scenario, but is being proven daily in corporations, divisions, departments and organizations all over the world.

The following outcomes are not only possible with a coaching engagement, but are actual outcomes from my clients and hundreds of other people who have participated in coaching. Imagine what your life would look like and feel like if you had the following characteristics:

- intentionally seeking feedback on your performance
- self-awareness that creates continuous improvement and change
- knowledge of weaknesses and strengths and the ability to work with them

- self-confidence
- positive self-judgment
- self-knowledge
- continued self-growth
- identifying and staying true to your values
- intelligence, talent, and skills
- surrounding yourself with other superior performers who challenge you
- knowing what you want and going after it
- a deep sense of caring for yourself, others, and the world
- giving back on a continuous basis
- a solid, caring, and loving family life

Of the hundreds of ways to improve your life, I have not seen or experienced a more immediate and effective way than coaching. My client testimonials make it sound like I walk on water, but it is really my clients who have taken the coaching principles and put them to such dramatic use in improving their lives and assuring they become superior performers.

Let me give you a few examples of how my last two clients were before they were willing and able to apply the coaching principles and methodologies to their lives.

Sam was hiding in one corner of his office when I first met him. He was the CEO and president of a 25-year-old printing company. Sam's company was not doing well. His staff was in disarray and confusion. The commercial lending bank that held his business note was calling him each day inquiring as to whether or not the company would be profitable again and when might that happen. Sam could not bring himself to return his customers' telephone calls. He had completely stopped meeting with his employees and barely even spoke to anyone at the office. And his personal life was suffering as well.

Beth had finally made it to manager within a very prestigious

corporation. However, Beth's ill health was disrupting her performance and progress at the office. She was unable to sleep for more
than two straight hours at night. Beth had developed panic attacks
during department staff meetings, and her attention to detail had
deteriorated.

Both Sam and Beth were in a heap of trouble personally and professionally and had no idea how to even begin to dig out from their
messes. When I entered the picture as their coach, they were both
defeated and were feeling hopeless about ever regaining their spark for
life and their superior performance edge.

Values, Purpose and Identity — Sam

Sam and Beth were experiencing what we all experience to some
degree when we are not honoring our values and working toward our
highest purpose.

In order to work well, you need to have clarity about the job to be
done. Sam had forgotten to create that clarity for himself, his staff, and
his organization. I asked him what were the three most important
aspects of his crisis that he would like to handle. He told me that he
wanted to become profitable again, create excellent and solid relationships with his staff, and put together a company-wide customer service
program that the entire company could support and participate in.

We began by defining how his goals would look on a daily basis;
what would have to be implemented in order for the goals to be met. He
began by calling his bankers and letting them know that he was putting
together a plan for profitability. Next he held a whole-company lunch
meeting and shared his thoughts about creating a superior customer
service program. He enlisted his staff in setting up groups to study the
situation and report back at a weekly staff meeting. He also set up individual and confidential private meetings with each staff member to
review profitability problems and his current action plan for creating

profits for the company. He asked for input from each staff member and set up a task force for profitability based on the comments from his staff.

As his coach I met with him on a weekly basis for six months; we talked on the telephone each week, and we communicated as often as he needed through e-mail, telephone, and fax. I was invited to the staff meetings to help give structure to the plans. Sam and I developed a bonus plan to be paid out when the company became profitable again.

Within two weeks, the entire organization was different. The atmosphere was positive and the people were more enthusiastic than they had been in years. Part of the reason for the positive energy in the company was the lack of secrets about the condition of the company and the enlistment of everyone in the reinventing of the company.

Why such quick and outstanding success? Who waved a magic wand over Sam to get him to do what needed to be done? What Sam did was not magic, but strategic and based on his highest values.

—He defined the problems

—He determined what high-value results he wanted, based on his purpose, vision, and identity

—He defined, designed, and implemented that which would create the greatest value for the organization, stakeholders, and himself

—He did what he was good at and what fit his values and purpose

Values, Purpose and Identify — Beth

Beth and I started working together exactly at the right time for her because she was not going to be able to work much longer if her health issues did not improve. In the previous three weeks, she had not slept for more than three hours a night, and it showed.

In our first meeting it was imperative to find out why she had gone from being a healthy, happy, and effective woman to someone who would have passed for a zombie. We were able to determine a few critical issues that she would need to clear up immediately.

Beth was reporting directly to the president of the firm. He was a self-made executive with little or no education and was proud of saying he had achieved his success with little help from anyone. When he promoted Beth, he had not defined her duties and had not made it clear what he expected from her. Every time he spoke to her, he would give her additional projects, and Beth never felt she could let him down by saying she already had too much to do.

Beth was completely unaligned with her own integrity because she had forgotten what was important to her. And she was kidding herself by thinking she had to be like her boss, the president of the company, and do everything without help — especially not asking for help.

Beth and I were able to identify her top values, which were commitment to doing a job well, contributing to the success of the company, and enjoying raising her dogs.

Beth needed to set up a meeting immediately with her boss. That meeting would define his expectations, her responsibilities, and a system of communication. This process would allow her to know what his expectations of her were, what her management job entailed and to set up a communication system with him. That would allow them to determine the most important aspects of the work he assigned to her and to set up priorities of the tasks to be done. He was very supportive of Beth defining her priorities because he respected her work and had become concerned about her health.

Within three weeks Beth was able to honor the schedule she had designed and to complete her management duties while also working on the special projects from her boss. She was also able to apply the new communication model to other parts of her professional life and was able to ask for help when the workload was out of kilter.

And she was able to resume entering her dogs in regional dog shows and actually won a couple of ribbons. She is now a happy, rested and proactive lady.

So what did Beth do to create such immediate results? No magic here either. She did the same thing that Sam did. She created a plan based on her values, purpose, and identity and what would bring the greatest value for the organization, the stakeholders, and herself.

Why It Sometimes Has To Get Crazy Before We Take Action

With the crazy schedules we keep, including 250 e-mails a day, child care issues, health issues, boss and organizational issues, sometimes we don't even know we are in trouble until there appears to be a big wall right in front of our noses.

We just keep moving along at a breakneck pace, thinking that the more we do, the more we will get done. Most times the problem is that the more we do, the more we do. Without a clear, concise agreed upon daily, weekly and yearly plan based on our highest values and purpose, we will continue to just keep doing until something brings us to a screeching halt.

Inside every superior performer are talents that are aching to be used: God-given talents that fuel our passions. We have dreams, desires, hopes, insights that need to be acknowledged and given a place to happen.

If we only spend our days doing, the talents get sidetracked into the place of "someday." Well, someday is today. Roll up your sleeves, take a big breath, and watch out because you are about to develop a plan for your own greatness — and it's not only about what you can get done.

What Do You Love?

What do you love? What do you value? What brings a smile to your face and a sweet feeling of accomplishment to your heart? Is it returning 250 e-mails a day? Is it having 16 projects on your desk to complete without knowing what they are for and why you are doing them?

Do you know what you want from life? Many times my clients cannot answer that question, but they surely can tell me *what is missing from their lives!* So what is missing from your life? Write a list this minute of the top five things missing from your life, and I will tell you what your values and purpose are. Are you missing:

—more time with family

—creating a great workplace and job satisfaction

—making more money

—a great relationship with a superior human

—sweet friendships and spending time with them

—travel to foreign lands

—a better relationship with God or Spirit

—the ability to really contribute to your work environment rather than "doing stuff"

—reading, gardening, puttering around

Wheel of Life Exercise

How smooth is your ride through life? Complete the exercise at right and immediately see how your life might not be working as well as you would like. Fill in the wheel and see how your ride might be.

Wheel of Life Exercise

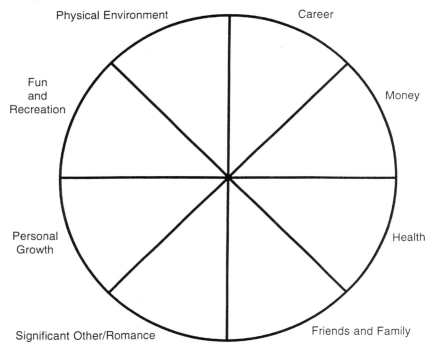

Directions: The eight sections in the Wheel of Life represent balance. Regarding the center of the wheel as 0 and the outer edge as 10, rank your level of satisfaction with each life area by drawing a straight or curved line to create a new outer edge (see example). The new perimeter of the circle represents the Wheel of Life. How bumpy would your ride be if this were a real wheel?

Example

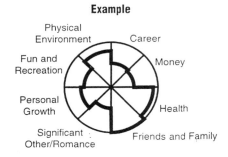

The wheels are used with permission.

So what do you want to change? Are you honoring what is most important to you in your life? What is missing for you?

And how smooth is your work life? Take the quiz below and see where you might want to make changes in a not-so-smooth ride.

Management Competencies Wheel

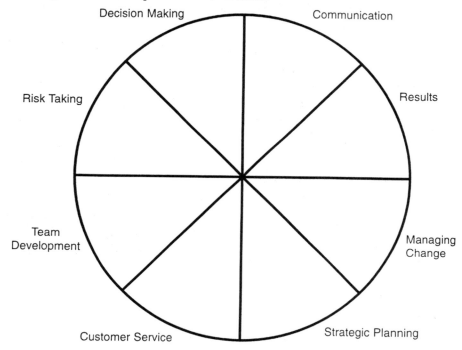

Directions: The eight sections in the Wheel of Life represent balance. Regarding the center of the wheel as 0 and the outer edge as 10, rank your level of satisfaction with each life area by drawing a straight or curved line to create a new outer edge (see example). The new perimeter of the circle represents the Wheel of Life. How bumpy would your ride be if this were a real wheel?

Example

Results You Can Expect From Executive Coaching

Sam and Beth are not isolated stories of superior performers gone wrong in their working environment. They are real people who had the very real issue of not recognizing their values and purpose in their life and not having a plan to realize them.

Organizations can be changed. Departments redesigned. Managers and executives can become extraordinarily effective because of executive coaching. By answering the initial assessment questions, you can begin to see where the value of executive coaching lies. How would you answer these questions yourself?

1. What is the result you want to produce within the next _____ (period of time)?
2. What strengths or assets do you have that will support you in accomplishing your results?
3. What challenges or liabilities do you have that can be an obstacle in accomplishing your results?
4. What else is important to know to support you in successfully accomplishing your results?

By spending time with these questions, you can begin to see what is important to you and who you are.

Executive coaching helps you to orient yourself to what it is that you want and to begin to see what your "vision" of life is and how it would be possible to achieve it. Your coach will help you navigate through developing your goals, mission, and strategies and will help you clarify why those components are important to you and the process.

You will begin to align your foundation and to determine if you have designed results that are most important to your bosses, peers, customers, and yourself. And are your results consistent with your most positive and powerful drives. You and your coach will begin to notice patterns that are either strengths or challenges and how to work with them, and will learn how to share those concerns and overcome them.

You and your coach will determine what driving forces are impacting your strengths and how to keep them positive. You will also learn how to change through the limiting situations and to mitigate the impact of the disempowering situations.

Clarifying the outcomes that you want and creating high-value relationships and results will become stressless and habitual. You will be able to easily identify the most important measurable results and to achieve them. And while all of these patterns are being established and used, you will learn to leverage your strengths and handle your limiting patterns because you will always be working from what is most important to you — you will be living and developing your life from the place where your highest results originate — your values and purpose.

Benefits From the Executive Coaching Relationship

It's obvious that the coachee is a beneficiary of the coaching engagement, but look at who else benefits:

—the organization gets a committed, focused, enthusiastic employee
—the coachee works from a place of high purpose and clearly defined goals, mission, and outcomes
—the subordinates and co-workers benefit from the high value and integrity generated by working on the real issues and the issues that are most important to all concerned
—relationships flourish because high-value relationships become the highest expectation of all involved.

Real People Testimonials

"I did not know that I could be this effective, rested and happy."
— Beth S. Portland, Maine

"My boss told me I was going to be coached. It was not something

I wanted because I thought it meant something was wrong with me. Guess what. There was. I was lost, angry, inefficient, and hiding behind ignorance of what was important. It's all changed. I feel great and I work great too." — Marc E. Newton, MA

"After owning my own software company and being leading edge in all technology sectors, I thought I knew it all. My coach helped me align what was most important for profitability and it was lots more than marketing and sales. Don't let your ego stand in the way." — Ray W. San Diego, CA

"My personal and professional life changed dramatically. I was able to finally have a personal life, make money, vacation, and begin to write articles for my industry. High-value relationships developed through values, and defining my purpose allowed me to have a full and prosperous life." — Tina S., M.D., Concord, NH

Radical Results with Loving Actions

So what do you want in your life? Implied in that question is "What is missing for you?"

I've spent the last 15 years of my life as a single parent, business owner, and leader in my community. It was not until 1993, when I took on my first coach, that I realized that I was living a very limited outlook. It was my way or no way. My coach helped me recognize what I wanted, who I was, and how I wanted to live my life.

I love life and I wanted to live it fully. Raising my kids. Making money. Supporting great clients in their dreams. Giving back to the community. Raising the most beautiful peonies in New England. And I did and I have.

Having a coach has meant that I have tripled my income; produced international products; have been on TV and radio; have great children who are healthy, happy, strong and delightful; my home is beautiful; I am healthy; I have the best friends in the entire world, and my relationship with God is sweet and strong.

Don't wait one minute longer. Go back and do the Wheel exercises and see where you are out of kilter in your life. Then get on your computer and write me a note. I will help you develop high-value relationships with yourself, your professional life and your community

The best is yet to come!

I send you my love, Natalie Manor

The Definition of Executive Coaching
from ICF Conference October, 1999

Executive Coaching is a facilitative one-to-one, mutually designed relationship between a professional coach and a key contributor who has a powerful position in the organization. This relationship occurs in areas of business, government, not-for-profit, and education organization where there are multiple stakeholders and organization sponsorships for the coach or coaching group. The coaching is contracted for the benefit of a client who is accountable for highly complex decisions with wide scope of impact on the organization and industry as a whole. The focus of the coaching is usually upon organization performance or development, but may also have a personal component as well. The results produced from this relationship are observable and measurable, commensurate with the requirements that organization has for the performance of this person being coached.

"Wheel of Life" exercise from *Co-Active Coaching* by Laura Whitworth, Henry Kimsey-House and Phil Sandahl, 1998, Davies-Black Publishing (used with permission).

High Value Relationships — with thanks to Steve Lishansky, President, Success Dynamics and the Executive Coaching Institute.

ABOUT
NATALIE MANOR

*N**atalie Manor brings clarity and leverage to her clients and audiences by providing the means to develop extraordinary high value relationships both personally and professionally in order to become superior performers in all areas of their lives. She is an executive coach, consultant, speaker, and author. She offers powerful, practical and on-target advice for mastering executive and team excellence, executive skill building and communication. Natalie also instructs on corporate workplace issues, with an emphasis on developing executive women. Her KICKS audio tapes have been endorsed internationally in publications such as* Entrepreneur, Self, Runners World, USA Today, Kiplinger's, Prevention, Men's Health, *and* Paul Harvey's Report. *She has appeared on BBC's AllNight and on hundreds of radio and TV stations. Natalie stays current with memberships in the National Speakers Association, International Coaching Federation and American Society for Training and Development.*

Contact Information:
Natalie Manor
Natalie Manor Associates
P.O. Box 1508
Merrimack, NH 03054
Phone: (800) 666-2230
Fax: (603) 424-1267
E-mail: CoachNatalie@manorevents.mv.com
Website: www.NatalieManorAssociates.com

CREATING VISION-LED SUCCESS

by Tom Guzzardo

Introduction

In the midst of busy lives, turbulent change and no job security, we each seek a life of significance, order, and meaning. Do you ever ask yourself if what you're doing with your life really makes a difference? Why is my personal life so hurried and fragmented? Why isn't there more love and support in my marriage/significant relationship? I assert that we seek to have lives of purpose and meaning beyond our busy schedules, individualistic desires, and self-absorbed lives. We can generate true significance and meaning by finding a true sense of vision and purpose for our lives.

Late in the afternoon of October 6, 2000, 27 men and women met in the Atlanta airport as Jack Till briefed us on what to expect on our mission in Nicaragua. He told us the next ten days would be long, hard and hot, as we would be laying concrete block walls for three buildings for an orphanage. After an eight-hour flight, we landed in Managua, Nicaragua. The next morning, Jack, our project manager, had us up at 5:30 a.m. and at the job site at 7:00 a.m. The work was intense, back-breaking labor, in 90° heat, and the tropical sun. Jack was hardworking, encouraging and always in the middle of the most physically demanding tasks.

By the end of the day, we were all drained. On the bus going back to the hotel, that night, Jack shared with the troop, "I really appreciate your hard work and commitment. You've got to see the bigger picture. We are not building three dormitories for the children left homeless by the recent hurricanes, we are changing the lives of over 50 children and their families for generations to come. By loving and serving these people, we are changing spiritual landscapes of Central America." Jack Till retired from IBM at 52 to lead mission trips to Central America. He has more energy, passion and joy than any 25-year-old I know. He is a person who's living his vision, mission, and "calling" simultaneously.

We have all heard stories of people like Jack Till. These people seem to have a clear sense of vision and mission for their lives. These people have an increased focus, passion, power, and ability to get results. Many leadership and personal growth books tell us the value of having a personal vision and business mission statement, but nobody tells us how to discover our vision for our personal and business lives. Let us examine a process to generate a vision for your life and an inner call that can yield a true sense of clarity, significance, and meaning.

Basics For Success

I define true success as creating and living a "wholistic and Spirit-led vision" for your life. This vision reflects your highest values, missions, and dreams. It creates balance and wholeness as it encompasses each area of your life. The vision is guided by your inner voice and led by the Spirit of God.

In my business and coaching practice, I coach and work with people who pursue a "wholistic"and Spirit-led vision." I refer to these people as "Partner Leaders." I call them Partner Leaders because of the strong partnerships they create with their families, business associates, and community and the leadership they must show in living true to their vision. Partner Leaders generally report that their vision: 1) gives them real significance and meaning, 2) is a Spirit-led "calling" to a certain career, personal relationship, and community project, and 3) creates balance and wholeness as it encompasses each major area of their lives. "It was like something bigger than myself led me to this work and job. I have an inner knowing about my key projects and relationships," confided Tim Hockman, one of my clients.

Finding Your Vision in Four Areas of Your Life

Your vision will address one or more of these areas of your life: 1) Meaningful work, 2) Personal life, 3) Family and loving relationships, 4) Serving others/leaving a legacy. One key to success is finding balance in all of these areas of your life. Often people seek greater clarity and purpose. They pick one or two areas in which they sense a "missing" or "yearning," and they work on these areas. What comes to mind when you think of a real "missing" or "yearning" in your life? Write it below. There is no wrong answer. (We will be referring to this later).

_____

_____

_____

_____

_____

For example, a person in his 20's, focusing on his career, seeks to define what he wants to do with his career and find a really meaningful job. Three years after a divorce, a thirty-five-year-old single mom begins to yearn for a special person with whom she can share her heart and life. A person in their 40's, after achieving their initial career goals, seeks more fulfillment and reevaluates what's important. Something is "missing." See where your "missing" or "yearning" shows up in one or two areas of your life.

Meaningful Work

Partner Leaders generate and live a vision of meaningful work. They report that they are able to use their true abilities, gifts, and skills in work that they find to be truly meaningful. Through the work that they do, they live their highest values and feel that they are truly making a difference. Their work becomes a "mission" with urgency and power. They feel called to serve a particular group of people with specific needs. Partner Leaders use their unique gifts to serve these people and truly make a difference in the lives of these people.

"I had already achieved a lot of professional and financial success by age 44. Yet I sensed there was more for me to do. As I looked deeper I connected with a new group of people, I could really help through my financial planning practice. The business vision we developed created a new level of focus, energy, and creativity for my work. I feel younger, more alive, and excited about my work than I have in years," shared Steve Leshner, a client from Philadelphia.

Personal Life

Partner Leaders live meaningful personal lives. They develop their personal goals, priorities, life roles, and key play projects. They create their own criteria to measure their success. They ask themselves, "Am I living my highest values in family, partnership, health, and spiritual growth?" "What's really important to me? How can I grow in my character, i.e. having peace and integrity?" They report experiencing inner peace, love, and acceptance for themselves and for the people around them. [I want to add a note of caution: this is not a constant experience but a frequent occurrence in their life. Living one's "calling" in every area of life is an ongoing process.] They have lives of balance and they often feel whole and complete in themselves.

Extended Families/Loving Relationships

Partner Leaders give love and support and create connection with their immediate family. They also include a "created extended family" of very nurturing people and relationships in their lives. Their "created extended families" become their support system and their chosen partners to expand in growth and development. They are able to love and see the best in others.

Helping Others/Leaving a Legacy

Partner Leaders are people with a "calling." A "people," a "cause," or an "issue," can call them to serve. For example, a person can be called to work with teens in the inner city, or work with young children who have cancer. Partner Leaders help others in need out of their commitment to touch the lives of others. They often describe this commitment as having a "ministry," or a desire to give back to their family, profession, church, synagogue, or community from which they have received blessings. They report, "I receive a deep sense of meaning and significance, that comes as I give to others who have no ability to give back to me." Partner Leaders are involved in projects that benefit others and that will outlast their lifetimes.

Cliff Louvette felt a "calling" to start a support group for fathers. He focused on fathers being more supportive, consistent and loving with their elementary school children. Once a month, men came together to share, learn, and discover new ways to love and support their children. Cliff said that bringing men together to learn to better parent, love and support their children became a huge desire. He enrolled a team of men to support his vision. The idea took off. The group now has more than 100 men attending each month from all over Atlanta.

Finding Our Vision:
The Spirit-Led Discovery Process

In a recent conversation with my fiancée, Kathryn, she asked me, "How do you find your vision for your life and your work? How do you discover what you are to do? Where should you serve?" I shared with her that finding our vision begins with a "yearning" for more. We feel a desire for more meaningful work or sense emptiness or "missing" in our personal lives. We seek more connectedness and sharing with our family or extended family. Often there is a desire or concern to help others with a particular need.

Through a process of discovery, dying to ourselves, and inner guidance and Spirit direction, we birth a new vision in our lives. There are stages in this "Spirit-led discovery process":

Stage 1: Surrendering,

Stage 2: Listening to the Spirit,

Stage 3: Hearing counsel of wise people,

Stage 4: Knowing,

Stage 5: Being in action.

Stage One:
Surrendering

We must die to self and old patterns as we prepare the way to find our vision. The first part of this stage is *cleansing and purifying*. In this stage we let go of the past and the things that keep us from seeing a new vision. We forgive other people and ourselves. We release fears or barriers to the Spirit. If you're seeking a new relationship, the past relationship needs to be completed, forgiven, and released. There's a process of "letting go" and creating a vacuum that allows a new vision and way of living to emerge.

A Prayer Of Letting Go

"God, I don't know what You want me to do. I am confused and

fearful about my future and 'missing' what You have for me. Forgive me for being so selfish and shortsighted. I find it hard to trust You and others. Guide me to the things You wish me to do. Show me the person You wish me to be. Light my path that I may see where You would have me to go and serve in Your Spirit. I yield myself to You."

The second part of this stage is *yielding*. We yield old beliefs, habits, and patterns to create a new future and possibility. We create something new, like writing a whole new chapter of our life on brand new paper. We create from nothing. If we have had a number of unfulfilling love relationships, we must cleanse the past and let go to create a new possibility and vision of a new, loving relationship. This stage is characterized by an unknowing, waiting, or an openness to what is new and possible. We cleanse, heal, let go, and wait for a new vision and model of living to emerge.

A Prayer of Yielding

"Thank You for the gift of another day. As I go through the day, help me to see how I can serve where I am. Show me what I must learn and what I must release so that I can move to the next level in fulfilling the vision You have for my life. I trust in You to move through me as I keep my heart open to You."

Stage Two:
Listening to the Spirit

In this stage, Partner Leaders sense a new vision for the possibilities that can be in their lives. Through prayer, journaling, reflection, being in nature, being still, they are able to sense and see a new vision and possibility for their work or their personal lives. For Mac Schneider, a client, a vision for a new personal life of peace, integrity, and health emerged that created a new level of energy, focus, and productivity.

You may be asking yourself, "But how do I sense this vision? People discover their vision by "seeing it," "hearing it," or "feeling it."

People who are largely visual learners learn best from seeing and writing things down, seeing a bright new future. "I had a vision, I could see myself doing an exciting new work." People who are auditory learners, who learn best by hearing and learn well by listening to tapes, told us they hear an inner voice. "I could hear an inner voice guiding me to work with that new project." Kinesthetic learners, people who learn by feeling, by doing, and by intuition, seem to sense their vision. They get a feeling in their body of "the rightness" of a possible future. They often hear the question, "How did you know that he or she was the right one for you to marry?" and their response is often, "I just knew. I had a feeling inside that this person was right for me." This process of listening to the Spirit evolves over a couple of days to a couple of months. What emerges is a clear new vision that is "heard," "seen," and "felt" that people can verbalize and share with others.

A Prayer of Listening

"God, help me to sense Your guidance and leading. Help me to know the difference between my desires and wishes and Your true 'calling' and guidance. Help me to be still, hear Your voice, and sense Your Spirit and wisdom. Show me my new path. I walk by faith and Your guidance."

Stage Three:
Hearing the Counsel of Wise People

People in our community often see us more clearly than we see ourselves. People will speak to us about our gifts and what they see as possible. They might say, "You're really excellent at speaking and entertaining; have you ever thought of being a professional speaker or entertainer?" "You have a natural gift and love for organizing parties and people. Have you ever thought of being a meeting planner or owning a catering service?" Be open to the wisdom that your community and people who know and love you can contribute to guiding you to your vision.

Partner Leaders ask two or three mentors to guide them as they seek a vision for their work, family, or leading a legacy project. They speak to each mentor separately to get independent counsel and to create ongoing support and accountability. "Help me clarify what's right for me as I seek a new career." "Help me discern, is Jack really the right one for me to partner with? I'd like your guidance." The counsel of at least two independent people and their broad perspective guides us in finding our higher truth and clarifying our vision.

Stage Four:
Knowingness

After cleansing, prayer, meditation, and the feedback and counsel of wise people comes clarity of vision. You know and sense the vision. Partner Leaders say, "Yes! This is a person I can see myself partnering with in business." "Yes, this is a project that really calls to me and speaks to my heart." "Yes, I know I will marry him. It feels right." People usually describe this experience as a peaceful inner knowing. They have increased focus, energy, and power. Jan Russel, a client, shared, "After five months of struggling with my vision for my business and my personal life, I could feel the Spirit guiding me to specialize in a new business niche. I sensed a new desire to love and support my spouse. I felt a new clarity and joy about my work and my relationship."

Stage Five:
Being in Action

In the first part of this stage, the clarity and energy to create an action plan naturally emerges. After much reflection and seeking, we now are guided to the right people and the next steps emerge smoothly. We find ourselves focused, energized, and naturally attracting the resources, people, and ideas we need to implement the new vision. "My fiancée and I decided that we wanted to take a trip to Italy. In the next two days, we were magnetic to the resources we needed. We talked to strangers about our vision, and they shared with us their experiences of their travels to Italy and gave us two travel books on Italy. I found magazines in the dentist's office that talked about great spas in Tuscany and the culinary delights of Rome." The vision now has a life, power, and attractiveness of its own. Partner Leaders, at this stage, are guided by the Spirit on how to accomplish the vision and mission.

The second part of this stage, *taking action,* seems to occur naturally. There is peacefulness from within as you are drawn to the vision. This vision is something you would truly love to accomplish. Partner Leaders work on their vision and take consistent action as they are guided daily by their inner voice on ways to accomplish their short-term goals and vision. They report, "There's a sense of focus and ease, while moving toward accomplishing this vision. We are able to create and adjust to the changing circumstances, as we move smoothly toward our vision." When there are barriers and breakdowns, they ask themselves, "What do I need to learn? What's my next step?" As they stay focused on the vision it draws them and they do whatever it takes to move toward it. There seems to be a gentle balance between doing and being as they continually ask, "What am I committed to? What actions do I need to take to accomplish this vision?"

Jack Hughes, a financial service client, reported, "Over a couple of months I felt uneasy about my career and personal life. My management team was dropping the ball on some important projects, and the company had three unprofitable months in a row, which was scary. I was busy doing paperwork and solving minor service problems, not getting to serve my 'A' clients or coaching my top sales people. I felt really frustrated and drained. I was not getting any exercise, was cranky, and a pain to live with. I began to ask myself, 'Am I in the wrong profession?' I sought the counsel of my pastor and I hired a professional business coach. My prayer was, 'God, guide me; do you want me to stay in this career? What are my lessons? What are You trying to say to me?' Through my business coaching we were able to identify my highest values, unique gifts, skills, and the projects that really energize me. We clarified, 'I am a visionary, a teacher, a team builder, and an encourager.' I needed to let go of a lot of administrative tasks and other people's monkeys and projects. I prayed and journaled and listened over the next four months. A new vision emerged. I took a leadership role in my business, formed a new management team, and began a ministry to teenagers at my kid's school. As the vision became clear, I had a new clarity and peace. I felt energized. The goals and projects to which I needed to commit became very clear. The action plan to move forward was equally clear. I was really excited about the new direction and enrolled others in working with me on the projects. Each day I pray and receive guidance about what is and isn't important. I have a new peace, and I sense the Spirit guiding me throughout the day."

You might be saying to yourself that sounds too simple and easy. This "Spirit-Led Discovery Process" is a natural, organic process and it is best walked in faith with the support of close friends and the counsel of wise people. One of the pitfalls I have experienced in seeking a vision is that I must let go of my ego and my ability to "figure it out." Our fears raise their ugly heads and must be confronted. My fears are "I'm not good enough, what if I fail and look really stupid?" This "Spirit-led Discovery Process" is filled with faith versus doubts, surrender versus trying to be in control, and fear versus the courage to keep going. Although this process is simple and predictable, it is not easy for any of us. The Spirit will lead you if you surrender, listen and trust Him.

Practical Application/Implementation:
Finding Your Vision

How can we apply these ideas of creating a vision to our personal lives, meaningful work, family/extended family, and helping others/

leaving a legacy? Let me give you a simple process and practical questions to ask yourself. We implement the following process with our business and personal clients: 1) ask yourself empowering questions that create focus; 2) pray, reflect, and think about these questions; 3) write a journal, collage a picture, walk in nature and reflect on your answers to these questions; 4) get feedback from your counsel of wise people; 5) allow time to reflect and integrate (repeat Stages 2, 3, & 4); 6) clarify as your vision emerges.

Finding your vision and doing "The Spirit-led Discovery Process" requires: 1) courage to create something out of nothing; 2) blocking quality time to reflect, pray, and review; 3) good support and counsel from your counsel of wise people; 4) trust that the Spirit is loving and guiding you to your vision and mission. Let's apply this to your life. Remember the "missing" or "yearning" in your life that you wrote down earlier. What was the "yearning"? To what area(s) of your life does this "yearning" relate? Ask yourself these empowering questions right now: 1) What would I love to create in this area of my life? What would this new desired life look like? 2) Who do I choose to be? 3) What do I choose to do? 4) How can I serve and benefit others with this vision? Over the next few days begin writing a journal, do a collage, and allow time to reflect on the new vision you would like to create. Trust that the Spirit is living and will guide you to your vision.

Practical Actions to Create
a Vision for Your Personal Life

Here's a sample exercise on creating a vision for your personal life. Allow time to write your answers and reflect on these over the next week. Ask your counsel of wise people to help you clarify your ideas and vision. Then take your ideas and answer the questions from the exercise. Trust the process and the Spirit to guide you.

1. My *highest values* are: (e.g. health, teamwork, mastery, creativity, play, joy)

_____

_____

_____

_____

_____

2. The *character qualities* I wish to live out are: (e.g. integrity, peace, service, persistence, consistency, accountability)

_____

_____

_____

_____

_____

3. My *unique gifts* are: (e.g. painting, listening, encouragement, organizing, solving complex problems)

_____

_____

_____

_____

4. I use my unique gifts by doing *key projects of service*:
   (e.g. teaching teenagers, building homes for the homeless,
   leading men's groups on fathering skills, fundraising for
   children with cancer)

_____

_____

_____

_____

_____

5. Actions to take to create *life balance* are: (e.g. aerobic exercise,
   healthy eating habits, time to be alone to reflect and nurture,
   quality time with spouse/significant relationship, growing
   spiritually, creating adventures)

_____

_____

_____

_____

Vision for my Personal Life

Fill in the following questions. *Be honest with yourself.*

I. I am a _____ person.
(Character)

II. I use my unique gifts to: _____.
(Projects)

III. I do _____ to create life balance.
(Life Balance Action)

IV. I love creating a life of: _____.
(Values)

Illustration

I am a man of peace, power, and integrity. I use my talents of coaching, teaching, and leadership to empower my children, spouse, and best friends to have extraordinary lives. I regularly exercise, pray, eat healthy, and get support from very nurturing people to create life balance. I love creating a life of health, leadership, and personal growth.

As you do this exercise, allow time to reflect, get feedback from the counsel of wise people, and trust the Spirit to guide you. A bright new future and vision of clarity and power will emerge from this process and the Spirit.

Summary and Conclusion

True success comes in living a Spirit-led vision that reflects one's highest values, mission, and dreams. This vision creates clarity, passion, purpose, and peace in the four areas of your life:

- Meaningful work
- Personal life
- Family and loving relationships
- Serving others/leaving a legacy

In which area is there a "yearning" for more? Have the courage to take action and embrace the "Spirit-led Discovery Process." I encourage you to listen to your heart and "yearning." Try this process and let the Spirit guide you to new levels of living and serving.

ABOUT
TOM GUZZARDO

*T*om Guzzardo works with business owners who want to grow their businesses. Through consulting, coaching and development of educational resources, he partners with business owners and entrepreneurs committed to breakthroughs in their businesses and personal lives. Tom and his team, "the Partner Coaches," provide programs on Partnership Leadership, Quantum Business Growth and Life Balance & Mastery.

Regardless of the size of your firm, Tom Guzzardo get results. Tom and his senior consultants deliver customized training, seminars and keynote speeches that increase team effectiveness and productivity which increases profits.

Contact Information:
Tom Guzzardo
Guzzardo Leadership Group
109 Holly Ridge Road
Stockbridge, GA 30281
Phone: (770) 474-1889
Fax: (770) 474-0442
E-mail: Guzzardo22@aol.com
Website: www.TomGuzzardo.com

Wynne-Wynne Approaches to Valuing Diversity on Work Teams

by Anja Wynne, M.A.

Ten years ago diversity was not a buzzword. Instead, we lived with terms such as affirmative action and equal employment opportunity. Unfortunately, over time these words have become synonymous with each other. However, there is a distinct difference between the three terms, which may affect how you interact with your colleagues on team projects, day-to-day operations, or even in social settings.

The results of the 2000 Census are in and it is clear the face of America is changing; we are a more diverse population than ever before. There are eight major demographic shifts that affect all workplaces, some more than others. The shifts range from an aging workforce and an increase in the number of foreign-born and disabled employees to the issues that surround dual-income families and single parents. I submit there are very few places in America that could dispute these demographic changes. Upper New England may not experience shifts in ethnic diversity in the same manner as Central Texas or Southern California, but they certainly are experiencing the impact of an aging work force, while the automobile manufacturing industry, a traditionally male workforce, is experiencing the increasing number of female employees and work/life balance issues facing today's workforce.

As an individual, the way you define diversity will impact the effectiveness of your organization and your personal ability to be a valuable, contributing member of a team. It can sometimes be challenging to always keep an open mind and truly respect the opinions of those who differ greatly from you. The fact that America's population is so diversified adds even more potential for miscommunication and misunderstanding. I will focus on two demographic shifts, the increasing multi-cultural population and the increasing need for work/life balance, to demonstrate the role diversity can play in this new century. Both will provide great insight into issues that clearly impact each one of us as we interact daily with our colleagues.

Our Multi-cultural Population

Following the 1990 Census, 30 percent of the United States was comprised of multi-cultural citizens with the most prominent groups being African-Americans, Hispanic-Americans, and Asian-Americans. These figures continue to increase, and the 2000 Census further supports this trend. In fact, in 51 of the 200 largest cities in America these three groups represent the majority population. But if you live or work in a region of the United States that is not experiencing this shift in the population you may not find this information very useful.

When this same information is translated into dollars, everyone's ears perk up. The fact of the matter is the collective buying power of these three ethnic groups alone tops $500 billion a year. That is more than the individual Gross National Products of the United Kingdom, Italy, Canada, and Australia. During the past decades affirmative action plans dictated the inclusion of these citizens, but common sense says that inclusion is just good business sense. By recruiting ethnically diverse employees, targeting sales in culturally diverse marketplaces, and retaining the quality synergy that is realized by diversifying your business team, you are guaranteed to share a portion of the $500 billion.

But what happens when organizations rush in to capture their portion of this pie? If the intent is purely for economic growth, an organization can end up with just a few crumbs. If the intent is to truly grow with this opportunity, and embrace each and every team member as a contributor, then the possibilities are boundless. The challenge is to develop work teams that respect the organization's objectives, as well as the opinions of everyone on the team. This is sometimes easier said than done.

As with any work team, members bring their unique personalities to the meeting. Some are taught to be reverent around senior leaders, while others are taught to voice their opinions. Some are more comfortable reporting to the group verbally, while others prefer written reports. Add to the mix each individual's cultural or ethnic characteristics, and meetings can become increasingly more complicated. For instance, the Hispanic-American culture generally regards the opinions of older males with the utmost respect. Imagine the confusion this can cause when the team leader is a significantly younger female.

Another major obstacle in the workplace perpetuated by the ethnically diverse population of America is the language barrier. Many second and third generation American-born citizens are embracing their native tongue in an attempt to preserve a piece of their heritage. Asian-Americans are more likely than the other three groups to maintain a large, extended family under one roof, therefore increasing the need for fluency in their native tongue, as well as fluency in English. While it is widely recognized that English is the unofficial language of America, the debates regarding the use of other languages in and around the workplace can hinder a work team's progress. Since this is one of the most common cultural conflicts in the workplace, a case study addressing this issue follows.

CASE 1: *The Language Barrier*

Pete Kensley met with his sales team weekly to discuss goals and objectives for the quarter. His team was comprised of eight sales representatives, and their collective sales achievements had surpassed the national standards during the past three years. Due to the quality of his team, his meetings maintained a consistent agenda and were quite predictable. The team recognized this fact, and side conversations soon became the norm. While most of the members of the team contributed to the side conversations at one time or another, two of the sales representatives were less likely to contribute to the distractions. These two men were both Hispanic-Americans and chose to discuss their opinions between themselves during their breaks. As they both spoke Spanish in their respective homes, they frequently used Spanish during these discussions.

Throughout the year the team's sales began to slip. However, the two Hispanic-American males continued to meet or surpass the national sales average. The six other members of the team became frustrated with their declining sales and began to expend unnecessary energy analyzing the success of their two Hispanic teammates. They came to the conclusion that the two men were withholding valuable information from the team — information they shared during their Spanish-only break time conversations. The six representatives decided to approach Mr. Kensley with their conclusions, demanding the two Hispanic-American males refrain from using Spanish in the workplace. Mr. Kensley respected the wishes of the team and spoke to the two males. He explained that their use of Spanish in the workplace was disruptive and created a hostile work environment. The two men argued that they rarely discussed work-related issues in these private conversations, except to share notes on their experiences in the heavily populated Hispanic communities throughout the region. Furthermore, they spoke Spanish only during their authorized breaks. Mr. Kensley understood their argument and agreed non-work related topics could be discussed in Spanish during their breaks.

- Given that English is the most accepted business language in the United States, was it appropriate for Mr. Kensley to allow the two Hispanic-American males to use Spanish in the workplace?
- Should he allow Spanish to be spoken during authorized breaks?
- How would you respond to the remaining six members of the team?

Quality of Life and the Workplace

Key diversity experts, as well as the Census reports of 1990 and 2000, validate that women comprise 52 percent of the population. More importantly, their attitudes about working outside the home are changing. With this shift in the population comes an increased awareness of daycare issues, flextime, telecommuting programs, and the need for all members of the team to actively work towards removing the perception that barriers may exist which preclude a woman from attaining the position she desires. After all, it makes good business sense to keep 52 percent of the population on your side.

This increase of women in the workplace affects every member of the team. Naturally, the first things that come to mind are typical 'women's issues' such as maternity leave or caring for a sick child. But more and more men are requesting time off for family activities, assisting with the care of an elderly parent, or looking into telecommuting opportunities that will not hinder their professional careers. These are virtually the same issues that have affected females in the workplace for years.

Fortune 500 companies are recognizing the need to contribute to the work/life balance continuum. Ernst & Young, a professional service firm, predicted the shifts in the population. In 1996 they developed the Office for Retention in order to retain talented employees through flexible work schedules and by responding to the work/life issues that affected them. It is estimated the company has saved $17 million on the recruiting and retention of women since it developed the office. The company can also attest to drastic improvements in morale.

DuPont is another leader in recognizing the need to address work/life issues before they become a problem. During this time of such low unemployment rates, DuPont is able to retain employees by providing a broad range of programs that meet their varying needs. The company's philosophy is to initiate sound policies while the organization is thriving, rather than trying to take corrective actions after the fact. The company feels confident it is offering the appropriate programs; however, the focus is now shifting to ensuring that employees are taking advantage of the programs. Often, employees fear they will be looked down upon if they 'take advantage' of good programs. DuPont's answer to this is to lead from the top and make sure management is actively participating, too.

DuPont and Ernst & Young are just two examples of the hundreds of organizations responding to the needs of their employees. Unfortunately, not all companies are so proactive. For some it took the Family and Medical Leave Act (FMLA) to jump-start their programs, but in some cases even that is not enough. The FMLA is designed to help employees balance their work and family responsibilities by taking reasonable unpaid leave for certain family and medical reasons. It also seeks to accommodate the legitimate interests of employers and promotes equal employment opportunity for men and women. Many assume the Family and Medical Leave Act is another one of those 'women's programs,' when in fact the Act provides male employees the same opportunity to spend time with newborns or to care for a sick parent, and it restores his job after the leave period.

CASE 2: The Baby Case

Sharon Crosby was provided the opportunity of her career when she was appointed Team Leader, International Product Development. The team was designed to create a plan for introducing a new product line in the Far Eastern market in early March. Naturally, all the members of the team came highly recommended and were known to be innovative, hard workers. The project was on a strict timeline and the March 1 deadline was firm.

In early July, Harold Parker announced his wife was due with their first child in January, and though he had no accrued leave, he intended to take unpaid leave for the period following the birth. Ms. Crosby, being very astute, prided herself on recognizing the needs of her team members. She spoke to Harold, discussed his role on the team, and offered to modify his project assignment. Though he was selected to spearhead the final phase of the project, they agreed to frontload his work, so he could spend time at home in late January and early February.

By late August the team was running into minor complications, none of which would greatly affect the outcome of the project, but each obstacle created tension among the team members. It was during this time that Corinne Hasselford informed Ms. Crosby that she was pregnant with her fourth child and due in February. According to company policy, Corinne would leave work three weeks prior to her due date.

Ms. Crosby was faced with a dilemma. She had already accounted for Harold's absence in late January and modified his work schedule accordingly. But now a key player, active in the final phase of the product launch, was authorized by law to miss a substantial amount of time from work. Ms. Crosby had no choice but to revoke Harold's request for leave from the project until after March 1.

- Would you handle this situation differently?
- Does Harold have a valid argument for appealing Ms. Crosby's decision to revoke his approved leave?
- Who is covered under the Family and Medical Leave Act? Corinne, Harold, or both?

The Management Challenge

Both team leaders in the previous two scenarios were faced with complex issues. Whenever a team member is approached about something that affects them personally, emotions can get in the way of the decision-making process. However, as managers or team leaders there are many options available to you that will benefit the entire team.

Pete Kensley's challenge is rather common in today's workplace. As a manager, he acted appropriately in requesting the two Hispanic men limit their use of Spanish to non-work related topics during their breaks. It is important that Mr. Kensley explains his decision to the other team members and reassures them the team's goals will not be compromised.

Sharon Crosby's situation, on the other hand, is less common in the workplace. Both Harold and Corinne are eligible for leave due to the birth of their children. Under the Family and Medical Leave Act employees are authorized to take up to twelve weeks of leave, paid or unpaid, based upon their respective company's benefits package. Therefore, Harold could certainly appeal the decision to revoke his leave request. As a manager, Ms. Crosby should discuss a variety of options with Harold, including the impact of granting him his original request, and come to a joint resolution.

There are challenges to managing people who are different from ourselves. But there are three simple steps you can apply to each situation. First, acknowledge that differences exist. Then, educate yourself about these differences through reading, listening, and interacting.

Finally, work together to value each other's differences in order to achieve a win-win solution.

Food for Thought

Fours years after I worked with the United Nations in Somalia on the East Coast of Africa, my family moved to America's beautiful New England area where lobster is a staple, not a luxury. Virtually every Sunday we would go to the dock and purchase fresh lobster for dinner. In fact, our 3-year-old son learned to love and expect it, so each week I was reminded of my international lobster experience.

When in Somalia on a peacekeeping mission my role was to provide logistical support to a starving nation in civil unrest. Interestingly, of all the African nations Somalia has the largest coastal border, measuring approximately 1,700 miles, yet the Somali culture does not recognize the ocean as a primary source of food, nor has the government been successful trying to capitalize on the earning potential of a fishing industry. On a rare occasion a local Somali, wise in the ways of Western capitalism, would offer to trap lobsters, steam them, and sell them to us for a nominal fee. While we dined on the finest lobster of the Indian Ocean, the local nationals were starving due to drought and war. Though we offered the locals lobster and encouraged them to embrace the sea as a source of sustenance during this period of drought, we could not fully appreciate their long-standing tradition of raising goats and camels. Perhaps it was this cultural conviction that was one of the reasons the entire nation struggled with starvation.

Eventually the nation of Somalia turned around and was able to send an official delegation to the United Nations Conference 2000 in New York City. Looking back on that year, I realize it was a difficult lesson to experience, but in so many ways we learn this type lesson every day on our own work teams. The message is to recognize that we all have a value system that we live by, not right or wrong, just different from those around us. So, when in the presence of a multi-cultural team member or a colleague with significant family issues, just remember that some prefer goat to lobster.

ABOUT ANJA WYNNE, M.A.

A nja Wynne is an expert in diversity and social issues. She is a dynamic facilitator and practiced problem solver whose experiences span the globe. Ms. Wynne managed a workforce of 25 German nationals and 55 Americans while working in Germany, and worked with the United Nations as a Logistical Liaison Officer for the U.S. Army, meeting daily with representatives from 24 countries. She is a certified mediator and has assisted in resolving a variety of interpersonal conflicts, allowing organizations to focus on their bottom line. The NAACP presented the Roy Wilkins Service Award to her (as well as to General Colin Powell). Wynne, a Major in the Air National Guard, served as a national facilitator for the implementation of their new diversity initiative and has instructed at the Air Force Academy. Practical application of her problem solving techniques was demonstrated in the medical field when she joined Pfizer Pharmaceuticals as a consultant to physicians and group practices. The knowledge gained from these dynamic experiences provides a strong foundation for her customized workshops, invigorating presentations and application of experiential training.

Anja Wynne earned a B.A. in International Business and German at James Madison University in Harrisonburg, Virginia, and a Masters in International Relations at Boston University's Heidelberg, Germany campus. Additionally, Ms. Wynne attended the Defense Equal Opportunity Institute, graduating with distinction.

Contact Information:
Anja Wynne, M.A.
The Wynne Group
511 Impala Trail
Harker Heights, TX 76548
Phone: (254) 698-4826
E-mail: WynneGrp@aol.com

EMPOWERING
YOURSELF AND OTHERS:
MYTHS AND REALITIES

by Jim Hunt

If you picked this up thinking that it is probably more of what you have read before about empowerment, think again. There have probably been more words written about this subject that are not only wrong, but show just how little understanding there is about this subject, than almost anything I can think of. Why?

Money! Yes, money. Empowerment has been a hot topic and buzzword for quite a while. Here is how it works. Some recognizable name writes about the subject. People buy it not because there is necessarily any credible evidence that the author knows what he or she is talking about. They buy it because of name recognition! Author name recognition.

So what's the real story? Well, suspend if you will all you have ever read or heard about the topic and let's talk reality. First you have to separate empowerment of yourself from empowerment of others. One is a decision; the other, according to the so-called experts, is permission. Here is where we start to separate the truth from the nonsense.

First, let's talk about empowerment as it relates to empowering others. There is no such thing! When was the last time you empowered someone? Not motivated, not inspired, not encouraged but actually empowered them. Never! And it's not because you haven't, didn't or wouldn't want to; it's because it isn't yours to give. It's a decision issue, not a permission issue. Don't get tired of hearing that because the more you hear it and think about it the more sense it's going to make to you.

Empower means to authorize or to enable, both verbs. What this means for our purposes is that you can sanction someone to do something or give that person permission. What it does not tell you is whether or not the person is willing or able to take action on your permission. What we are able to do is to build the borders around or put the boundaries around what we believe we have empowered them to do. Both of these activities serve as guides but have nothing to do with willingness or capability.

Many times you hear empower or empowerment used as if someone had just been granted a wish or as if you had just done someone a favor. Often managers think they are using this as a reward when in fact it may feel more like punishment. Why? Because with or without permission, being asked to do something may raise doubts, fear and reluctance because of past experience.

One of the biggest challenges in many organizations is that how they do business is so steeped in their culture that you can talk until you are blue in the face about change and people just won't believe you. They see management come and go and they see "programs of the month" pass through, but fundamentally not much changes. That's because "culture eats change for breakfast" and there are probably many people who have a significant investment in keeping things the way they are.

The second factor is that "pain drives change," which is to say that unless the cost for doing things the way you are doing them obviously has become too high, and the cost for making the change is lower than paying to maintain the status quo, nothing is going to happen. And those that you are trying to change must realize that as well. They have been there, done that and even have the T-shirt. So here is the dilemma. You think that you have just given someone permission to act. When nothing happens or it doesn't happen on time, we assume that all we need to do is just to go back and reinforce the first message. Wrong! What needs to happen is for you to start asking some smart questions.

Was what I asked you to do clear? Was the timing clear? Do you have or are there any tools that we need to supply you in order to carry out the task? Is there any question as to the scope of what I have asked you to do or as to my authority to ask you to do it? Are you questioning whether or not you have the skills to do it?

People don't act for many different reasons that may be tied to the answers to those questions. But there could be another almost invisible factor at work here, and that is the culture. It could be that by doing what you ask them to do, the culture might in fact punish them. Sometimes, in fact many times, there are people in the organization who are so heavily invested in how things used to be done, that it becomes a threat to change them. They will go to any lengths in some cases to preserve the old ways.

A company I was working with thought it had found the perfect opportunity to change its culture and style of management. For almost a hundred years this had been a top-down, almost dictatorial place to work. Sound familiar? The CEO had retired and his replacement was named from within the company. He knew things needed to change but unless he was in the top spot he was in no position to do anything. But now he had the top job, and he went to work to change things.

He had committees working to put together a new plan for the company. He involved the employees and management both. He seemed to be setting the example of participative management. The committees did their work, the plan was put together and everyone walked away from the exercise feeling very proud of what had been accomplished. What happened was that every efficiency that could be effected by top management and the CFO worked, and the overhead came down and the savings went up. But almost all of the changes that depended on changing the style of management and increased participation by the employees foundered. Why?

Top management believed that by getting the rest of their management involved along with the employees, they were empowering both groups to go and do wonderful things. They weren't. It made them feel better, but the underlying problem didn't go away because very few believed that things could or would change. People who they thought they had empowered weren't. Most did not believe the message or they thought that it would not last. Management's fundamental error was in thinking that just because you give people the opportunity to change things, they will. They won't.

The message that things have changed, will change, or are changing has to be sent over and over and over again with substantial visible evidence to back it up. The United Way-like charts showed that savings were occurring, but the evidence that how we did things was fundamentally changing was missing. Conclusion: here we go again!

Even if the company had had its share of empowered people, the culture was so entrenched and the members of management so invested in the way things had been done before, the effort was stalled. The most empowered people in the world, when faced with this kind of situation, will do one of two things. Help change it or get out! The best way to lose these people is for good management to do nothing.

So what are the lessons to be learned? One, in an organization you don't really empower anyone; you just draw the lines for them within which they have to operate. Two, "culture eats change for breakfast" and a well-entrenched culture with people heavily invested in keeping it that way, for whatever reason, presents a formidable challenge to anyone who thinks he is going to change it. Three, a long-standing culture inadvertently or proactively encourages keeping things the way they are, and it will take several truly empowered people to change that culture.

When there is a change at the top of an organization it is the best time to change other things because people expect it. If you have really empowered people in the organization who have just hung in there for whatever reason, now is the time to take the shackles off and let them help you. Don't mistake this action for turning the prison over to the inmates; it's not. What you are doing is finally letting people unleash their promise and potential to help you do what you need to do. Then stand back, and watch the miracles happen.

Have you ever watched someone who seemed to have great potential not ever amount to a tinker's darn and someone who seemed to have the cards really stacked against him or her come out on top? It makes you wonder what it is that allows someone who comes from the poorest of circumstances, or who has a disability that would crush or stop most people rise to incredible heights in a vocation or in life in general. I did too, and it was that question that started me on a lifelong search for the answers.

I have had friends growing up who had all the advantages that a good and prosperous family could provide, and yet for reasons that up until now were a mystery to me could not get their lives on track. Even after they were picked up and helped time after time they still continued to seemingly sabotage any possible success in their life. It wasn't until I started learning from those who had made it, in spite of handicaps, that I began to learn why some succeed and others fail.

I am going to share with you the six keys that all of the people I interviewed and studied had in common and what those keys unlocked for them in their lives.

First, is how they viewed themselves. Without exception, the people I studied saw themselves as whole, complete, and unique as individuals. They believed that they were a perfect manifestation of the external power they believed in and relied on in the universe. They were able to separate the doer from the deed. When they didn't perform at the level they knew they could, they didn't start condemning themselves; they learned from their mistakes and got back up to try again. They weren't looking for scapegoats, escape hatches, or any other reason why they didn't make it work. Their attitude was one of persistence to keep going until they accomplished what they were after, or to stop and recognize that they had given their best shot and that they were OK with that.

Second, each of these individuals had somehow learned that each of us acts out our own script and that the script had begun to be written while we were children. The things that become a part of the script are often comments, suggestions, praise or criticism from those around us. I remember my second grade teacher once telling me that I would never be any good at math. She was right, or at least I made her right by making her prediction a self-fulfilling prophecy.

Empowered people know the truth about the script, which is if we are responsible for what we let become part of it, we can re-write the old one, and, in the case of someone who is really determined, write a new one. The messages that we got all those years that we listened to and made a part of our own script are there only because we allow them to be. So at any given time we can choose to ignore them, though it isn't always easy, and start to write a script of our own.

Another thing empowered people learned, especially about anything negative that could become a part of their script, was to deal with it promptly. For instance, if someone said to you "I guess you never will get the hang of this new technology," don't just accept that statement in a moment of frustration, but challenge it. Never accept anything anyone says about you that is negative. No one knows you like you.

Most of us have heard the axiom that " it's not what happens to you that counts, but how you react to what happens to you." As true as that may be, my interviews with truly empowered people suggest that they go one step further. In fact, empowered people anticipate situations and prepare ahead to deal with them.

I have coined an axiom based on my experience with these kinds of people and that is "the answer is not new when the question isn't either." In other words, if we have thought about how we would react if certain situations were presented to us and had already decided how we would respond, when they really happen our response has been rehearsed, if you will, and is not made solely on the emotion of the moment. Can we anticipate all or even most situations? Probably not. But that is not necessarily important. What *is* is that you have thought about your reaction to challenges to your values, morals, ethics, and anything else that would impact your self-perception or self-esteem.

You can write your own script for your life because I have seen people do it. The key is to have a written plan for your life, a LifePlan©. Most people spend more time planning a vacation than they do planning their lives. Here is something to remember. If you don't have a plan for your life, somebody else will. By not having a plan for our lives we hand over too much influence, by default, to others who may or may not have our best interest at heart. Here is an exercise that will help you focus on two things: One, your priorities, and two, getting a good start on writing your LifePlan©. On paper write down a list of all the things you would want to do if you knew that you had only one year to live. Take whatever time you need to make your list. Next, with your list in hand, make any changes you would need to if the one year turned out to be only six months. Third, take your six-month list and change it in any way you need to reflect the six months now changed to 30 days. Finally, make any changes to the list if you found out that you really had only one day.

I have used this exercise with all levels of persons in all types of organizations. Some of them have come to tears as they constructed their lists, realizing how little attention they had been paying to what they now say are the top priorities in their lives. Just think of it this way:

how would it change your everyday life if you were making all your decisions based on the priorities that remained on your one-day list. I have seen this exercise make some dramatic changes for people at all levels and from all walks of life.

Pain drives change at the personal level, too! Think about it. Whether we are talking about your diet, getting in better physical shape, getting out from under the person or company you work for, or even getting out of a destructive relationship, most people don't do anything until the pain of their current situation gets so high that they finally have to do something about it. Most people find it easier to adjust to a lower standard for themselves than to do the work it takes to make a change. Not empowered people.

Why do you think that there are so many self-improvement books and tapes sold, hype-type seminars gone to, and still so many people producing hardly any result? Let me share a staggering statistic with you. Of all the those books and tapes that people start to try to change their lives, fewer than two percent have been read from cover to cover or listened to from start to finish. Now why would they spend all that money and not finish them? Not only that but we also know that it is generally those same people who are out buying new ones. Without having finished the other ones!

I call this the "magic pill syndrome." People are always looking for that magic pill that will turn their life around, and most of them keep searching without even "taking" the pill or pills they had already bought. What empowered people know that others don't is this: The river of life runs with or without us. It doesn't care who we are, what our background is, or where we live. It does not discriminate. Everybody approaches the river of life looking for what can be taken from it. But what do they bring with them to fill?

Some people bring a teaspoon and some bring a cup. Some bring a bucket and yet others bring a barrel. The river will give and fill up whatever we bring to it. Then why do some bring only a teaspoon, cup or bucket when they could be bringing a barrel? It's because in their script over the years they have become convinced that they only deserve having one of the smaller vessels, or that because of who they are or where they came from they are not allowed to have the barrel. It's not true. Empowered people know that you can have whatever you want, but you can't have a barrel kind of life if you bring only a teaspoon to life. Decide today that from now on every time or every day you dip into the river you are going to do it with a barrel.

Another thing that the empowered person has learned is that most of the unhappiness we bring to our circumstances is brought by comparison. It doesn't or shouldn't make any difference what any other person in the world owns or has because that person is not you. That whole, complete and unique person that I mentioned earlier should be on his or her own unique path, not comparable to any one else's. Television advertisements, magazines and billboards are designed to accomplish just one thing and that is to make you dissatisfied with who you are or what you have and to make you want what they are peddling. Don't fall for it. You are better than that.

Finally, one of the really differentiating attributes of the empowered person is that he or she trusts gut feeling. Yes, I said they trust their guts and you should too. Think of it this way: for however many years you have been living, you have been a human antenna. You have been receiving signals from all around you, from your own experiences and from everyone else's as well. All of that experience has been assimilated into that wonderful computer that you have in your head, your brain. It is fantastic!

Have you ever been trying to make a decision and an answer has just popped into your head as if some mysterious force had prompted you? It is not a mysterious force at all. It is all those experiences from all those years being processed by that wonderful computer in your head and being brought to bear on the question at hand. And what do we usually do? Argue with it and try to figure out where it is coming from and generally not trust that this could possibly be our own powerful intuitive selves doing what we have always been capable of. Trust your gut! It won't let you down.

It's OK to be OK with who and what you are today; you don't need anyone else's permission to be exactly who you are right now. You don't need your spouse's, your boss's, your friends' or anyone else's permission to be you. The empowered people I have known in my life are very much at home in their own skin. You should be, too.

Here is what my experience has concluded about those people so many of us envy because we see them as the captains of their own ships who seem to be fully in charge of their lives. 1. The river of life runs with or without us. It is up to us whether we come to it with a teaspoon, cup, bucket or barrel. It will fill up what we bring. 2. It's not what happens to us that counts; it is how we react to what happens that creates or destroys our future. 3. If you don't have a plan for your life, somebody else will. Create your own LifePlan© and follow it. 4. Most unhappiness in life is caused by our comparing our lives to others. Stop it! You define yourself and let the world around you support your definition. 5. Pain drives change! Change is an inside-out job. The reason most people fail is that they are always waiting for help to arrive. The reality is that it was there all the time, within you. 6. Trust your gut. Allow all of those years of experience to work for you and quit arguing with yourself.

Inner change is a choice! Make it today, and your life and the life of those around you can never be the same again.

ABOUT
JAMES W. HUNT

*J*im Hunt, President, eChange2, Inc. brings a unique and varied back-ground to his consulting practice, keynotes and seminars, and executive coaching. He is a featured speaker on transformational leadership; princi-ples, practices and psychology of change; and coaching/mentoring for senior level management. He is co-author of the book, Software Engineering and C.A.S.E., Bridging the Culture Gap *published by McGraw-Hill. It is a template for change in a technological world. Jim has worked at many levels within the Fortune 500, the banking industry, tech firms such as Motorola, Texas Instruments and Raytheon. He has also worked with Boeing, Kodak, Ciba Vision, and within utilities, governments, insurance, healthcare, and education. He has written numerous articles and is a contributing consultant to* Fortune *magazine. He also has served as personal coach to CEO's in several organizations.*

Jim is an active member of the Institute of Management Consultants (IMC), National Human Resources Leadership Forum and the National Speakers Association. His mission statement for his organization is, "To see, nourish, inspire, discover and encourage the best in every person and organization."©

Contact Information:
James W. Hunt, President/CEO
eChange2, Inc.
P.O. Box 2726
Alpharetta, GA 30023-2726
Phone: (770) 751-8763
E-mail: JWHunt@eChange2.com
Website: www.eChange2.com

HOW TO BUILD TRUST

by Pauline George, M.Ed.

Have you ever thought about what it would be like in an organization or a life that lacked trust and respect? Let's imagine.

Everything would have to be locked all the time

No one would listen to anyone else

Conflict could never be resolved

You would never have surgery

Change would be a nightmare

The world would be full of lawyers

Policing would be where most time was spent

There would be little ability to influence

People would be suspicious and unreceptive to ideas, proposals, and goals

All decisions would have to be made in a vacuum

You could depend on no one for help

And on and on. Trust is the reciprocal faith in the intentions and behaviors of others. Without it life would be a nightmare. Have you ever worked for a person you didn't trust? Do you remember how stressful it was to monitor everything you said and did? How you were never sure how or if your ideas would be received? The drain of energy and motivation you felt? How you felt yourself becoming apathetic?

On the other hand, what a wonderful existence when trust is present. When you can depend on people to support you, to do what they say they will do, and to empower you. I have worked for clients without a contract because trust was present. I have let people work in my house when I am absent when trust was present. I let vendors and contractors make strategic decisions for my business because trust is present. I have delegated major responsibilities with phenomenal results because trust was present. Trust is hard to describe; however, we know when it is present and we know when it is not. Trust comes from character, not a technique. You must be authentic, a person of integrity. That is, what you say lines up with what you do, lines up with what you feel, and lines up with the vision you are communicating. You must honor your commitments and promises and be ethical in all your relationships. Trust is that essential building block of positive relationships. Isn't that really what life personally and organizationally is all about?

One demonstration of trust happened in my life when I was directing a Canoe Camp. I became involved with a wilderness camping effort that took teenagers on varied weeklong adventure trips. I chose to direct an 88-mile, five-day trip down the New River in West Virginia in packed canoes. The 88-mile stretch included shooting rapids, one canoe at a time. That means you make a plan with your canoeing partner on an exact strategy and then you totally trust that the partner will follow through on the plan. No person alone can steer the canoe safely through rapids of the class we were encountering, loaded with supplies of food, clothing, and shelter. It meant I would do my part, believing that my partner also wanted to navigate that rapid with the intention of safely advancing down the river in an efficient manner. That experience was true learning in the power and necessity of trust in any relationship, no matter the river in life or work being navigated. In moments that really mattered, I needed the support and co-operation of a partner I could depend on. How sweet it was to have a partner I could trust and how disastrous it could have been without a trustworthy partner. What experience did you think about as you read my story that either represented the existence or the lack of trust in your personal life or at work?

I'd like you to think of one of the most significant positive relationships you currently enjoy, personally and/or professionally. Jot down a name or two. Now think about the ingredients of that relationship. I'll bet three of those ingredients are trust, respect, and support because they are the basis of every positive relationship. We realize that trust does not come naturally. People must want it and work hard for it.

Trust does come easier to some people than others. It is somewhat a factor of our behavior style. The naturally relational style which tends to be social and people-oriented tends to trust easily, while the analytical, task-oriented, and more assessing style views life critically and tends much more towards skeptical behavior. This style does not want to share information until certain of its accuracy. They are private people by nature. To build trust, people of this style need to appreciate the need for two-way communication in relationships. They need to choose to give more feedback regarding thoughts and feelings. Effective communication can be a desirable training for them. Which style do you tend toward?

This leaves us with the question: If you want trust, how do you live and work to get it? Trust is difficult to achieve and requires consistent hard work, for trust grows slowly and there is no speeding up the process. Building trust not only takes time but also physical presence and human energy. The good news is that when trust is present, differences that normally tend to cause conflict are valued and appreciated as strengths. People become more open and expressive, more frank, and more spontaneous. Conversation truly becomes authentic dialogue, and creative ideas are born. People feel comfortable, energized, and empowered. This desirable state is worth working toward.

Let's explore several characteristics and behaviors that enable people to build trust and respect.

Openness

Have you ever experienced an organization in which the leadership did not choose to either give or receive feedback? They may have even said that they did. I have been a part of such an organization but not for long. Leaders who work in secrecy and do not value the feedback of their people tend to have a revolving door — people come and people leave. This type of leader also misses out on many valuable ideas that are never shared, and, therefore, productivity is limited. It is unbelievably frustrating and limiting to work under leadership that is closed and uncommunicative. The same frustration exists in a personal relationship if high levels of communication, especially two-way, are missing. In fact we could ask, is it even a relationship?

To what extent do you share your honest thoughts and feelings in your significant relationships, personally and professionally? Or do you often keep them to yourself? Your answer is one determining factor in how open versus closed you are. Open people share their honest thoughts and feelings and are receptive to the thoughts, ideas, perceptions, and feelings of others. Think of the last time your boss, your spouse, your employee, or your friend asked you for your opinion on a pressing matter; were you appropriately open and honest? Or when you had some new and different ideas on a project, did you have the courage to voice them amidst differing opinions? Self-disclosure is a part of being open. People are more likely to be open with you when you let them know things about you and when you make yourself vulnerable by telling others about your own uncertainties and mistakes. Others need to know you are approachable and not averse to mistakes but accept them as a necessary part of creativity. Shared information contributes to trust between people. In order to create a climate of mutual trust, people must be appropriately open with one another. Think of communication and trust as being yoked together; they rise together, they fall together. The less communication, the less trust and commitment in any relationship.

Listening is also a part of openness. You can't be open without truly listening to other viewpoints, perspectives, and feedback with a flexible attitude that will enable you to understand and value diverse thinking. One must rise from a point of view to a viewing point to listen with understanding. Effective listening demonstrates respect and care, which build trust. The self-management competency must be used to listen effectively. Poet Robert Frost said, "Education is the ability to listen to almost anything without losing your confidence or control." Are you courageous enough to solicit feedback and listen just with understanding and not evaluation? At work are you courageous enough to have a feedback report solicited from persons you work with, for, and those that work for you? Are you open enough to review it without any other agenda but personal growth in mind? Try listening — it will foster personal and professional growth and you will be practicing openness.

Acceptance

Carl Rogers, the communication guru, found that the greatest barrier to effective communication is our tendency to evaluate. It is so easy and almost natural to make a judgment on what a person shares with us. That very judgment keeps us from an accepting and approachable attitude that is important when building trust and respect. To the extent I feel you will consider my thoughts as options is the extent to which I will trust you with my non-edited ideas. Acceptance is being non-judgmental, and being non-judgmental translates into certain behaviors. People listen to each other with understanding, mistakes are discussed and understood, and differences are accepted, managed, and valued. People are willing to dialogue in an accepting environment. Learning is valued and realized because we are open to new and creative thinking. In an accepting environment, people tend to reach higher levels of potential due to the freedom of expression and thought that acceptance fosters. Acceptance makes people feel safe and secure, which are necessary to develop trust. To what extent do you feel accepted in your current environment? To what extent are your feedback and ideas solicited and valued? To what extent do you accept differences and foster a feedback culture yourself?

Accepting people is very much an attitude, which is a powerful driver of human behavior because it is a choice. Although attitude is within our control, it is difficult to change when we have been practicing it a long time. Another piece of bad news is people are often unaware of the judgment they use when relating to others. It requires openness to become aware. Another way to define acceptance is the extent to which an individual respects and values diverse characteristics and behaviors of others. This is especially the definition used in diversity training and training involving cross-cultural differences. Two features of this perspective of acceptance are tolerance and respect. Tolerance relies somewhat on understanding and empathy, which are important factors in our attitude toward differences. Tolerance reflects how accepting one is of others who are different. When one is tolerant, he or she can accept the idea that all people should be allowed to reflect their uniqueness in their behavior. With increased tolerance an individual is open and relaxed when interacting with others. Tolerance grants others the same freedom of behavior and style that we expect for ourselves. Respect is dependent on high levels of knowledge and understanding on the part of the respondent. When one is respectful of others, he accepts them without compromise. Ultimate respect is seeing value in others regardless of their backgrounds. One's respectful views of other people are not blemished or tarnished by negative cultural or racial characterizations. When encouraged, respect creates change through trust. How well do you function in the acceptance of diverse individuals or groups? Do negative feelings ever prevent you from associating with someone or a particular group? Multicultural teams are becoming prevalent in the workplace due to the globalization trend of the new economy. Acceptance from a diverse perspective is crucial in building trust in these teams. Otherwise they simply are groups working together, and, therefore, they miss the potential benefits that diversity offers.

Predictability

Predictability refers to the degree of confidence that people have in their expectations about another person's behavior or intentions. When people have little confidence about how you will behave in certain circumstances, they may have hope but not trust. The gap that exists between what people expect and what actually gets acted out is a measure of unpredictability. In a poll of 215 companies, Manchester Consulting of Bala Cynwyd, PA found that the greatest trust buster was people acting inconsistently in what they say and do. People trust you to the extent they find you predictable and reliable or believe they can rely on you. Do you do what you say you will do? Some behaviors that act out reliability are that you are competent in your role, you help others when needed, you are punctual, you meet deadlines, and your responses in a given situation are predictable. Can you remember your last experience with an unreliable person? What happened as a result of that experience? Maybe you looked bad because he didn't do his part for a project or a presentation due. Maybe a customer was disappointed and let down because a deadline was missed. Maybe a business opportunity was missed because a proposal wasn't completed as needed. I know what I do. When I've experienced an unpredictable person, I tend not to involve or to limit the involvement of that person in future events or initiatives. I distance myself from that person as much as possible, and our relationship suffers.

Risk

Openness, the first characteristic mentioned, cannot exist without a willingness to risk. The risk is that a decision to trust can lead to either good or bad consequences. Trusting involves a certain level of vulnerability. Persons may take what you openly share and use it with other than pure motives. On the other hand, people who choose to play it safe really communicate an unwillingness to trust and therefore fail to generate trust. It all begins with the individual. This factor of risk is again related to the individual's behavior style, just like openness. Some of us are wired with a need to take risks while others have a need for predictability and stability, which prevent risk-taking behaviors that are necessary for building trust. As people demonstrate trust in other people, the response tends to reciprocate. It is worth the risk because without it you have no relationship. Do you trust your co-workers and others, believing that they won't let you down? Or do you play it safe, remain independent, and do it yourself or keep your feedback to yourself?

Depleted Trust

If you have ever read Stephen Covey's work, you recall he describes trust as a kind of bank account. In any relationship people begin with an amount deposited automatically. That account will grow in value as you behave in a consistent, reliable, and trustworthy way. However, minor acts of dishonesty and betrayal will whittle away at the account balance. You can find yourself in a condition marked NSF. This condition is critical because restoring trust is no easy task. Stephen

Covey says, "Trust or the lack of it is at the root of success or failure in relationships and in the bottom-line results of business, industry, education, and government." Unfortunately, trust can be demolished quickly and easily. A single act of trustworthiness does not outweigh a single act of untrustworthiness. When trust is betrayed, people take on self-protecting roles because hurt, anger, fear, and defensiveness arise. Rebuilding trust is a slow, difficult process. It is much better to not let it get depleted in the first place. Stephen Covey explains in *Principle Centered Leadership* that it is about trustworthiness at the personal level, leading to trust at the interpersonal level, being expressed in delegation at the management level, and alignment at the organizational level. That is worth working for.

Others' Thoughts

In the book, *In Search of Honor, Lessons form Workers on How to Build Trust*, Adele Lynn interviewed 1000 people to discover their perspectives on how to build trust in the workplace.

The employees interviewed defined four elements characteristic of trust. They are:

1. A sense of importance, directed at both the work and the people
2. Genuinely caring and treating people like human equals despite status
3. Expression of sincere gratitude and
4. Fair and equal contributions by employees in the workplace.

Underneath it all, says Lynn, the qualities of honor and integrity must be present in all interactions.

People want to be great. Trusting people means allowing them to be great. People want to live out their uniqueness. People search for opportunities to use their ability, their talents, and their ideas. People want a place where initiative and the willingness to take risks are rewarded with recognition and opportunity. A trusting environment provides for all of this.

Let's use the start, stop, and continue process to apply some action planning to what we just learned. In light of this information, what behavior and/or attitude will you start using that you currently don't use? Perhaps you will speak up the next time you are at a staff, board, or committee meeting with a crazy idea that you normally keep to yourself. Or perhaps you will attend listening training. You must be specific, and your plan must be measurable and timed to be effective. Secondly, what behavior and/or attitude will you stop because it is trust busting? Perhaps you will stop taking people for granted and make a plan to express sincere gratitude to those with whom you live and work. Again be specific. And lastly, what behavior and/or attitude are you currently practicing that is a trust builder which you want to continue?

ABOUT
PAULINE GEORGE, M.ED.

*H*er colleagues and clients describe her as inspirational, courageous, passionately knowledgeable, balanced and enthusiastic. Pauline George, M.Ed., is President of PG Training & Consulting and specializes in consulting, training, speaking and coaching to enable organizations to meet their staff development needs according to their mission, vision, values, goals, and objectives. Her passion is developing people.

Ms. George holds a Masters of Education degree from the University of Pittsburgh. Post-graduate she has studied adult learning, behavior science and group dynamics. She taught full-time at Penn State University for five years prior to beginning her own training and consulting business. A certified consultant for Inscape Publishing since 1986 (formerly Carlson Learning), she does extensive needs analysis assessments for each of her clients. Ms. George is a member of the National Speakers Association. Pauline serves on the board at the New Community Church of Wexford, PA.

Contact Information:
Pauline George, M.Ed.
PG Training & Consulting
1104 Forest Edge Court
Wexford, PA 15090
Phone: (724) 934-2836
Fax: (724) 934-2838
E-mail: PGtrain@attglobal.net
Website: www.PGtrain.com

SUCCESSFUL PEOPLE WRITE NOTES!

by Cecilia B. Grimes

S earching for that magic, sometimes elusive, formula for success? Wondering how some people seem to have it made — how some enjoy not just a mediocre measure of success, but success that could only be described as wholehearted? What makes one's success quotient rise and another's ebb?

It's an interesting question, particularly when "candidates for success" may start from the same square one: the right educational credentials, perhaps even fancy university degrees, steadfast commitments to success, substantial evidence of hard work that includes long on-the-job hours, even exemplary community involvement. Yet one fast-forwards past the other!

Consider that one may have a secret worth sharing: Successful people write notes!

They follow up dinner invitations with notes of appreciation to the hostess for the delicious food and fine hospitality, and for being graciously included in the guest list. They send sincere notes of concern when a friend or colleague sustains a loss, whether the death of a family member or the termination of a job. They proffer wholehearted congratulations through notes to celebrate the birth or adoption of a child, to provide accolades for a well-deserved promotion, to commend an inspiring presentation at a conference, or to heap kudos for a grand-daughter's game-winning free throw. To some, they forward notes containing newspaper clippings about a milestone in a friend or client's life — a copy of a profile featured in the business section of a newspaper, an engagement or wedding announcement, or an awards ceremony hosted by the Chamber of Commerce. To others, they send along a note sharing their grandmother's favorite pecan pie recipe, a powerfully penned poem that captures a unique thought or reverences friendship, a magazine feature on a topic of mutual interest, a recently located address of a long-lost friend, or perhaps a copy of an old photograph that's sure to recall a nostalgic occasion. In all these instances, these note-writers are proclaiming that they are aware of others, and they seize these day-by-day happenings as opportunities to extend themselves into the lives of others in caring, kind, thoughtful, and considerate ways. Let's call this an exercise in fine manners, and let's focus on note writing as the vehicle for building not only solid personal and professional relationships, but also for creating wholehearted success in the process.

The very power of this exercise in fine manners is that it's not mandatory: It is not a requirement! And that's its most powerful aspect: It is defined by a want-to element, not a have-to! Herein lies the secret of its ability to add another dimension to success. Wholehearted success!

What a secret to share — but surely one whose implementation might fill some people with trepidation. Before you dismiss this power-packed strategy for success as too time-consuming, too difficult, too demanding, too stressful, too much, read on. This chapter is for you.

Step one, however, does not involve writing.

You must accept the premise that successful people write. You must want to join their ranks.

You must want to extend yourself into the lives of others in order to build relationships that will enhance and complement your journey, and theirs, toward success by always being on the lookout for "fine manners" writing opportunities.

You must commit to a bit of discipline in undertaking to write notes, including learning about mechanics and structure and the importance of scheduling time to write.

You must adopt an attitude of *"This is not only something I can do, this is something I should do!"*

You must accept the fact that successful people write notes, and having signed on for all this, you must get ready to write before you write.

You'll need some writing stuff . . .

Step two is gathering your writing supplies. You'll need good quality papers, a writing instrument, preferably a smooth-flowing ink pen, an assortment of interesting stamps, and a standard dictionary. And you'll need to gather all these supplies twice. You can easily house the first set of these supplies in a handy, accessible area like a desk drawer devoted exclusively to this writing task. The other set should be portable so that you can carry it around. You'll be amazed at the number of opportunities you'll find to write notes while you wait for appointments or for flights. Use those moments to build your success quotient by dashing off notes of appreciation, condolence, gratitude, or congratulations.

You'll need to create a total visual package, inside and out . . .

The message conveyed in a hand-written note may be inside, but the outside creates the first impression to the recipient. A hand-written note is premier because it conveys a personal touch. You may elect to send your notes electronically. E-mail is widely used and certainly has its advantages. But it's the more labor-extensive, hand-written notes that impress the recipient. For our purposes, let's establish that you've decided to take pen in hand to write a note.

Let's look at the envelope first because it creates the first impression. Think of the steps in creating an envelope as a process of layering: the more layers, the better the impression. There are at least four components, or layers, to consider: paper, ink, address, and stamp. Neglecting any one of the four will diminish the power to impress.

If you choose to write on traditional stationery, select crisp, clean paper of a sufficient weight to feel impressive in the hand. A 20-lb. parchment works well; a 24-lb. quality paper stock is even better. If you wish to convey an environmental concern, favor recycled white or ivory. If you select the popular executive correspondence card, the paper weight will fall in the 40-lb. to 65-lb. range, and the size will be approximately 4 x 6 inches. (My personal correspondence cards are a bit larger and measure 5 1/2 x 7 1/2 inches. The stock weight is 80-lb.) Add another layer to the process by choosing black ink. Save the ball-point pen for casual writing.

For the outer appearance, most writers choose a block alignment featuring no indentations for the address. Begin with a designated title (called an honorific) for all addressees, whether Mr., Miss, Ms. or Mrs. Don't neglect this courtesy: Every person to whom you address a note should have the courtesy of a honorific.

You may correctly address an envelope to members of the medical profession with a first and last name followed by their appropriate degree, as in M.D. for a physician and D.D.S. for a dentist. Addressing an envelope to a member of the academic community who holds a doctorate would follow the same protocol, with a first and last name followed by the appropriate degree designation, as in Ph.D. (A comma always separates the last name and the degree.) A pastor would be titled "The Reverend." Elected officials at all levels, whether mayors, judges, town or county commissioners, governors, and members of Congress, should have "The Honorable" precede their names. Miss is correctly used until the age of 18; thereafter Ms. is used. (In the business arena, Ms. would be the correct honorific for a woman, regardless of her marital status.) Master is correctly used for young boys until the age of 10. Here are some examples:

- The Honorable Joseph M. Buckner
- The Honorable Don Lee Paschal and Mrs. Paschal
- The Reverend Joseph W. Casteel
- Alaina Budd, M.D.
- Jonathan Hedrick, D.D.S.
- Dr. and Mrs. William Clyde Thomas
- Charles L. Carroll, Ph.D.

To ensure the envelope's first-class appearance, select a stamp that is both interesting and scaled appropriately to the size of the envelope. This step is most easily accomplished by buying an array of stamps, several dozen at the time, of varying colors and sizes, and reflective of a wide range of interests. Selecting stamps of cartoon characters for children, roses for gardeners, and legends of baseball for athletes adds a special dimension to a note. Occasionally spend a little extra time at the stamp counter (skip the postal machines on this trip) and amass a stash of stamps that will add visual impact and importance — another layer — to your correspondence.

Take a look through your most recent stack of mail. Didn't the slim envelope that felt weighty in the hand get a bit of extra attention? Didn't you pause when you saw your name handsomely hand-addressed in ink? Wasn't that large, colorful stamp eye-catching?

Which envelope in the stack did you open first?

You'll need to follow some general guidelines
to give appealing form and structure to your note . . .

There are five components — or layers — that give appealing form to the layout of the message within: crisp margins, a first-line date, proper salutation, carefully aligned paragraph indentations, and a cordial closing.

Observe crisp margins all the way around — to the left, to the right, to the top, to the bottom. Avoid writing all the way to the edges. Matching up margin widths adds symmetry to the note's appearance. A half-inch margin to the left begs a half-inch margin to the right. Placement of the words on the page takes a little forethought, but visually it makes an important statement.

Provide a date, whether a general reference such as Thursday morning (most commonly favored for purely social notes that are sent expeditiously) or a more specific one (for the less expeditious writers among us) including the month, day, and year. Place the date on the first line of the note in the upper right hand corner. The right margin that you observe for this date is especially important because it establishes the margin for the rest of the note.

Begin each note with a proper salutation or greeting, include an honorific if appropriate, and follow the name with a comma. The first letter of the salutation establishes the left margin of the note. Its placement is important because the subsequent sentences of the note should rigidly follow this same left alignment.

Indent the first sentence in the body of the letter. The first letter of the first word should align exactly under the first letter of the name, or six spaces in. (The automatic tab for indentations on old-fashioned typewriters, way back when, was five spaces — four spaces for the word Dear and the requisite one space between words. The first letter filled the sixth space. The tabs programmed on today's computers generally are wider and perfectly acceptable for computer-generated correspondence.)

Align the closing with the date on the first line. The first letter of the date and the first letter of the first word of the closing should line up exactly. A comma follows the closing. Be particularly careful with the following popular and appropriate closings, as they include three of the most misspelled words in the English language:

- Sincerely, (9 letters)
- Yours truly, (5 letters, no apostrophe + 5 letters, no e)

The signature that concludes a note is written directly under the closing. If the note is to someone with whom you are on a first-name basis, then a first-name-only signature is appropriate. If you want to retain formality, sign both your first and your last name. Do not, however, give yourself an honorific. The courtesy of an honorific is conferred to others by you, but never to yourself. Any honorific designated for you personally should originate from others. (That also applies in introductions.)

You'll need to be conversational in tone . . .

The note should appear spoken rather than written. Phrase the message as if you were talking to the person. This approach removes the stiffness and formality that often plagues notes.

It's perfectly acceptable to punctuate loosely, using dashes and exclamation points. It's also fine to use incomplete sentences, as long as the thought is logical, because that's how conversation goes.

You'll need to exhibit good grammar . . .

It isn't necessary that you master the conjugating of a verb in its many tenses or know many impressive words in order to write a powerful note. What is important is reasonable attention to grammar. What should be avoided is the sullying of any note with misspelled words and grammar faults.

Be particularly on guard concerning homonyms (their, they're, and there; to and too; its and it's) that easily confuse, as well as the increasing misuse of the apostrophe. Possessive pronouns (theirs, yours, ours) never contain apostrophes, even though they show possession. Nouns, on the other hand, do use apostrophes (children's toys, Charles's award, baby's name) to show possession. Contractions (it's for it is; there's for there is; haven't for have not) always use an apostrophe to signal the absence of a letter.

Also be aware of pronoun selection in some prepositional phrases. Correctly you would write "for Carter and me," rather than "for Carter and I." (The technical explanation is that the object of the preposition requires an objective case pronoun. You'll easily correct yourself if you remove Carter and listen to the awkward and incorrect phrasing "for I.")

Don't guess at spelling. Use a dictionary.

Here's a quick reference on some commonly misspelled words:

- Congratulations has no "d"
- Ninety has an "e"
- Sincerely contains "e" twice
- Receive uses an "e" before the "i"
- Truly has no "e"
- February contains "r" twice
- Grateful has an "e"
- Recuperate has only one "a" but uses "e" three times
- Definitely uses "e" twice and "i" twice
- Separate has an "a" on either side of the "r"
- Acknowledgment and judgment both drop the "e" before the suffix "ment"
- Regardless is correct; irregardless is incorrect.
- "All right" and "a lot" are spelled as two words.

Wordsmiths like Gloria Gaither and William F. Buckley have glorious commands of the English language, but it's not necessary that you share their particular talents for inspired phrasing or impressive vocabulary. Do, however, strive for a higher level of articulation. Use words like appreciate, appreciation, grateful and gratitude to express thanks. Replace the handy, but over-used adjectives — nice, good, great, wonderful — with more expressive words. Your hostess will be thrilled to hear that you considered her dinner party delightful, rather than nice; the banquet table of food sumptuous, rather than good; the conversation stimulating or captivating, rather than great; the whole occasion (to which she has devoted three weeks of her life) inspired, rather than wonderful.

Infusing your writing with occasional alliteration (repetition of consonants in two or more neighboring words) will also add a bit of rhythm to your writing. Listen to the alliteration in golfing greats, fabulous fudge, wild and wonderful. Goodness gracious; inject some alliteration!

You'll need to send the note within a reasonable time frame . . .

That's probably around a week. An ideal would be to send a note within 24 hours of an occasion, but in the real world, that's often unrealistic. Do remember this truth: The longer you wait to write, the harder it will be to write. Other things will constantly compete for your time and your attention. Fresh proximity to the occasion is your best impetus to write; procrastination, your surest enemy.

Think of promptness as a virtue, a very impressive virtue. Schedule writing time: Successful people invariably do.

You'll need to focus on the recipient (the friend, the colleague, the client), rather than on yourself . . .

The best way to ensure that you tilt your remarks to the recipient is to start your note with you or your. "I want to thank you" tilts the note initially toward the writer; a reverse of the emphasis will capture the reader's attention more readily. Remember each writer should remember, "It's more about thee, than me!"

If there's a secret to writing effective notes, it's this . . .

To engage any reader, you must include *details, illustrations, and examples* within the note. Their inclusion makes the writing easier for the writer and infinitely more interesting and intriguing to the reader.

The absence of specific details, illustrations, or examples relegates a note to obscurity.

Details, illustrations, and examples are a must for a well-written note. Mechanics and structure are important, but they serve only as a framework in which to showcase a well-crafted message. It is your ability to tell a story, make an analogy, or re-frame an incident in an interesting context that will set your writing apart from the more mundane, generic grouping of flat, uninspired, predictable thoughts that so often pass as a basis for notes these days.

A note of condolence to a friend who has lost her mother:

July 15, 2001

Dear Diana,

Your mother was an inspiration to us all! My most fond memory of her centers on all those eighth-grade birthday parties at the Club Diane where she would gleefully watch us while we learned to "fast-dance." No one could ever forget those trays of fabulous fudge brownies she kept hauling to the refreshment table! She'll be missed not only by you and other members of her devoted family, but also by your growing-up friends on South Second Avenue to whom she was dear, and enormously kind, and a "dancer's" delight!

She will always be remembered because she was so well-loved. Her life touched us all.

With sympathy and warm regards,

A note of gratitude for a household gift:

February 1, xxxx

Dear Dr. and Mrs. Scheetz,

You have recalled a lovely memory for me with the gracious gift of pale yellow towels.

My grandmother used to hang pale yellow towels by her kitchen sink when she made her famous homemade breads. Now you, in your thoughtfulness, have provided me with a similar set that will repeatedly recall for me those precious memories of warm yeast rolls rising in her kitchen, more often than not with a pale yellow towel draped over the bowl.

What a very special gift!

With gratitude,

A note of congratulations to a client who has received an award:

June 26, xxxx

Dear Ed,

You make us all proud! The Governor's Award of Excellence stands within this state as THE outstanding tribute to a person who has distinguished himself or herself in volunteerism. Your devotion to Boy's Hope has been inspiring to your friends and colleagues, a source of pride to your family, and a life-changing contribution to young people. Look at the change in young Jeffrey's life — his is a heart-warming example of a "before and after" encounter with a caring adult.

We all want to make a difference. You truly have!

Sincerely,

Success means different things to different people. For many it's the achievement of lifelong dreams of prosperity — a fine home, plenty of money in multiple bank accounts, and a bulging stock portfolio. For some, it's prosperity of a different sort: a close and loving family, warm friendships, and meaningful, but perhaps not lucrative, work. For others, it may be measured by the depth of spirituality or by the presence of good health and physical fitness. All these perspectives embrace forms of great wealth and define aspects of success and successful people.

However you define success, remember there's a place within it for the exercise of fine manners.

Begin by devoting a portion of this week to note writing. Find three worthy recipients and compose a few sentences to each. This exercise will provide you with opportunities to acknowledge your ability to create a joyous moment for another. Claim a bit of your busy schedule to lift others up, to delight them, to surprise them, and to honor them with your written word. Enjoy immeasurably the relationships you will strengthen and energize.

Share with your favorite teacher a note about a special memory associated with your school years. Commend the wait staff at your favorite restaurant for their superb service at the corporate holiday party. Dash off a note to a grandparent who years ago, perhaps even decades ago, said the right thing at the right time when everyone else was critical. Write the mother-of-the-bride a note outlining the joy of the wedding — and especially write that note if you're the bride or the groom! Compliment the building attendant for his attentiveness, the meeting planner for her attention to detail, the chef for his magnificent creme caramel, the colleague for her remarkably researched and rousing professional presentation, the soloist for her enchanting music. The praise you confer as you move down receiving lines, the compliments you extend to colleagues in the hallways, the congratulations you offer at the conclusion of the awards banquets are lovely gestures. But if you really want to make a powerful statement, put the words on paper to do it! Not only do the recipients have the pleasure of a special kindness, they retain, in hand, a tangible reminder of your fine manners — one which they may surely decide to keep or to share. Soon enough, you'll understand the dynamic. The good you do returns to you.

Remember the road you are traveling to success will be made smoother, the trip kinder, the journey infinitely more exciting if you incorporate one basic, foolproof strategy for becoming successful: Write those notes!

Note Writing

General Guidelines
- Select clean, crisp, quality paper.
- Use black ink.
- Observe strict margins — top, bottom, left and right.
- Include a complete date at the top right side of the note.
- Begin the note with the proper salutation followed by a comma.
- Indent your first sentence, beginning directly under the first letter of the name.
- Keep the message within the body of the note short, cordial, and courteous.
- Project professionalism by focusing on the friend, colleague, client or patron, rather than on yourself.
- Provide details, illustrations, or examples to lift your note's impact and appeal.
- Include a correct closing, but be careful in its spelling.
- Pay close attention to grammar.
- Include an honorific when addressing the envelope.
- Toss out notes that contain smudges, mark-overs, or whiteout. Begin again.
- Remember the hallmark of a first class note: it is one the recipient wants to keep or share!

ABOUT
CECILIA B. GRIMES

*C*ecilia Grimes — author, speaker, trainer, and coach — is a certified etiquette and protocol consultant. She travels throughout the U.S. and works with individuals who want to present themselves with authority and confidence and who wish to add polish to their professionalism. Her clients include executives in Fortune 500 companies, athletes and coaching staffs, and professionals in the fields of engineering, law, banking and finance, academia, hospitality, and technology.

She is a native North Carolinian with an undergraduate degree from Wake Forest University and a master's degree from Duke University. She received her etiquette credentials at the prestigious Protocol School of Washington®. She is a member of the Carolinas Speakers Association, where she has served as hospitality chair, and the National Speakers Association.

Contact Information:
Cecilia B. Grimes
Etiquette Matters
513 West Glendale Street
Siler City, NC 27344
Phone: (919) 742-3616
E-mail: EtiquetteMatters@mindspring.com
Website: www.EtiquetteMatters.com

MAKE THIS
YOUR SMARTEST YEAR YET!

---

by Doug Smart, CSP

I have a friend named Mike. He lives in Metairie, Louisiana. As a storeowner he got to know many of his customers well. One man always asked Mike for a discount. Being a good businessman, he smiled, but it really bugged him. One day Mike asked the customer, "Why do you keep asking me for a discount? It's not like you need the money. You've got eight rental houses!"

The man smiled a sheepish grin and replied, "You can't blame me for asking. And besides, wherever I shop, I always ask for a discount."

"Does it work?" inquired Mike.

"Sometimes," he replied. "About ten percent of the time I get a discount."

Mike was amazed.

Does that mean you or I can walk into a store like Sears, Macy's or Dillard's, ask for a discount, and expect to get it? Sometimes! The clerk might look at you like you just fell off Jupiter, but don't be surprised to hear, "Well, okay. I'm empowered. At least that's what they tell me. I can make decisions. Come with me. We'll ring it up." And presto! It works! You know the old wisdom, "You don't ask, you don't get." Let me ask you something. In order for you to enjoy wholehearted success, isn't asking vital to getting? For example, if you are leading a sweeping

change in your company, such as implementing important new proce-
dures, don't you have to ask your co-workers to stay focused and
flexible? If you are introducing new products, don't you have to ask your
customers to trust you and try them? If you want to see improvement in
yourself, don't you have to ask yourself to be dedicated and determined?

Here's a quick true/false quiz:

In order to enjoy wholehearted success . . .

    ☐ T ☐ F You have to ask yourself to be open to new
          information.

    ☐ T ☐ F You have to ask other people to believe in you.

    ☐ T ☐ F You have to ask yourself to believe in yourself.

    ☐ T ☐ F You want to cultivate a deep appreciation for what
          you already have.

    ☐ T ☐ F You have to ask yourself to try new ideas.

    ☐ T ☐ F You need to find ways to keep your energy fired up.

The answers to all are true. Asking yourself to be strong in these
personal areas boosts your personal energy. To put a name on it, let's call
what keeps your energy levels high your rocket fuel, or RF.

In 1963, when President John F. Kennedy asked the American
people to accept his vision of a man on the moon by the end of the
decade, he was really asking for the energy that comes from commitment to hard-held goals. He did not ask if it were possible (which is a
good thing because the answer would have been impossible. At the time,
the scientific community did not possess even fifteen percent of the
information needed to accomplish the goal). He just asked us to believe
that his vision was possible. From the energy of that belief came the RF
to do the impossible.

You and I regulate our RF every day through the constant stream
of conversations in our heads. On a typical day we talk to ourselves
approximately 10,000 times. However, for many of us, it is estimated as

much as eighty percent of those personal 10,000 conversations have a negative tone, such as: "I can't. With my luck it'll probably rain. Nothing like that works for me." As adults, sometimes we are P.O.W. (Prisoners of Our Wishes). We get so bogged down in the impossibility of our challenges we drain off much of our RF, and what is left is diluted and polluted. Our rocket does not rise to the clouds, much less to the stars. What can we do?

I am a motivator, keynoter, consultant, author, and entrepreneur. After presenting over 1,000 presentations for organizations as diverse as Wal-Mart, Special Olympics, and the Kennedy Space Center at Cape Canaveral (hey, I have worked with real rocket scientists!), I have observed first hand that the people who seem to be secure, positive, and happy are the ones who maintain high levels of energy, confidence, and resiliency. They seem to manufacture their own RF. You can, too, with a formula for staying strong, confident, and resilient no matter what life throws in your direction.

10-20-30-40-50 Resiliency System

It's a smart idea to read for 10 minutes every morning. Ever wake up to chatter or music on the radio? Ever have the first song of the day stick in your head and you can't get it out? You're OK if it's a happy, upbeat song. But what if it's one of those depressing, spirit-draining, heart stoppers? Just as newly hatched ducks experience, early images imprinted onto an awakening brain tend to stick. Instead of gambling that good-for-you stuff will happen to stimulate your mind, take charge. For ten minutes every morning, it's a smart idea to read. Fill your head with things beneficial to you. Grab something to read that is inspirational, motivational, or "how to." For me, I love to read biographies — how did other people fight the lions, tigers, and bears of their lives? I'll grab a computer magazine. I'm not particularly computer literate, so I'll read an article to learn something new and maybe risk trying it out during the day. Or I'll grab a seed catalog. I love to garden, and it is spring in my house any morning I choose. I think that seed catalogs are the most optimistic literature on the planet — packed with optimism and the empowering message, "You can grow this, too!"

You have heard the old saying, "We become what we think about," so I urge you to take control and start your day thinking of things that are beneficial to you. It is smart to put wholesome brain groceries in your head for a fresh start. Begin your day in a strong, positive way. Ignore the TV, radio, and newspaper until later — all you'll miss is a diet that might be setting you up for feeling down. And avoid getting dependent on outside media to jumpstart your feelings anyhow. Instead, take charge and read for ten minutes every morning. It's a smart start to a terrific day every day.

Spend 20 minutes a day around positive, motivated, optimistic people. They can be an instant energy source for you. And if you can't find any, go rent some! Check out motivational tapes from your training library. Motivational tapes are popular listening for success-minded people as they drive to work.

Denis Waitley, author of *The Psychology of Winning*, says, "We become the people around us." You and I want to embrace the company of people who are good for us. We want to be around people who have the energy and enthusiasm for life of a nine-year-old. Christine, our nine-year-old neighbor, crossed the street and asked, "Can I catch bugs in your garden?"

"Sure, Christine," I replied, "but why don't you catch the bugs in your garden?"

"Because my Daddy sprays," she informed me, "and he says you don't. Last night he told Mom again that the big ones must still be coming from your side."

I still chuckle when I think about it. Isn't the openness of a child refreshing? Doesn't it feel good to be around adults who still have that frankness, optimism, and energy? Don't we need to be around people who speak their minds and don't play politics or wear masks? Go find them because life does not necessarily bring them to you. Haven't you noticed that if you do not go find the good ones, the bad ones fill the void?

Other people add to or deplete your RF. You know how you feel around people who gripe and moan about how life is unfair, work stinks, and that nobody really understands them. Depressed and de-energized come to mind because they contaminate the RF. On the other hand, when you are around upbeat people who volunteer for new assignments, put in extra hours to do something well, or enthusiastically help others reach their goals, you feel renewed and re-energized. Your RF is pure and increasing in volume. Spend twenty minutes a day around optimistic people and feel their energy and charisma arc into you. Enjoy them, let them flourish in you, and arc your spare RF over to somebody else.

Say 30 positive things about yourself to yourself every day. On a typical day we say 10,000 things to ourselves. Make at least thirty of them positive self-statements to build a supply of self-generating RF.

Saying positive affirmations about yourself is powerful. Three thousand years ago King Solomon noted that as a man thinks, he becomes. How often do you affirm the best in yourself? I recommend to all business people to say thirty positive things about yourselves to yourselves everyday. You want to say things that reflect your deep inner truth. Most will start with "I am." On my list I have: "I am a child of God. I am a good father. I am a doer. I am optimistic and enthusiastic. I am lucky. I am a risk-taker so that I gain security. I am an internationally known motivational speaker."

All that sounds very straightforward, but I'll tell you, it took me three months to make the list. When I first wrote down those things, I did not totally believe them.

The acid test is this: Read your list every morning while standing in front of a mirror. The hard part will be not flinching. You see, there are six billion people on Earth and you have the ability to lie to every one except one. Who's that? Yourself! If you flinch or avert your eyes, then you do not yet believe what you are telling yourself.

I want you to write out a list of thirty positive things about yourself that express the real you — both the way you are now and what you believe you are capable of becoming — and then every morning stand in front of a mirror and say those things to yourself. It's an emotionally healthy and powerful way to affirm your personal truth that your business life may have buried deep under the layers. Bring it back up. Live it!

Say "Thank you" 40 times a day. Zig Ziglar calls this "the attitude of gratitude" that affirms life is good right now. You and I have low-energy people on our teams who don't appreciate how good they have it. I suspect they see life as a stream of aggravations, challenges, and annoyances that have to be endured.

I was standing on the curb outside the Fayetteville, Arkansas, airport while I waited for a hotel shuttle to pick me up. A bright red car screeched to a halt just a few yards past me. The driver, obviously in a hurry, jumped out the second it stopped. Without looking, he reached behind himself to shut the car door. Like an errant baseball batter, he swung hard, but he totally missed the car door. He froze. His face distorted into a look of total aggravation. He stepped back, grabbed the car door at the top corner and slammed it shut — as if he were teaching that car a lesson. Then with a sour look, he stomped past me into the airport. I was just standing there on the curb with luggage at my feet waiting for a hotel shuttle, but, instantly, I felt a sensation come over me. I knew it was coming and I tried to resist, but I could not. I felt sorry for whomever it was he came to meet! There was someone in the airport excited to be coming home or arriving for business, and he was what awaited that person. I then thought, even if he were running late, he could have been grateful he could leave his car right at the entrance to the airport terminal.

Compare that incident to this. My plane landed in Dallas, Texas, at noon on a very hot day. When I went to get my rental car, instead of standing in long lines at the counter, I went right to the car lot. As a frequent customer, I have a card that allows me to skip the lines, proceed to a special area, and choose any car there. The paperwork is on the front seat and the keys are in the ignition. A guard checks me on the way out. It is a great system.

On that particular day, before I chose a shiny new car, I looked up at the exit and I could not help but notice there was no guardhouse. I did not see anyone to check my paperwork. "They sure are trusting in Dallas," I thought. I selected a beautiful new car, still wet from being freshly washed despite the intense heat. I backed it out, put it into drive, and as I approached the exit, I noticed a car parked on the side. Someone in a uniform was in it. The motor was running and the air conditioning was on. The guard apparently had helped herself to a new automobile, and she was using it as her office to keep cool. That had to make for a challenging day!

As I approached, a woman with a beautiful, energetic smile leapt out of the car. I pressed the brake, pressed the button to roll down my window and, without thinking, the first words that tumbled out of my mouth were, "It sure is hot out here. It must be rough working in that car all day." She looked down at me, smiled broadly and said, "It's not so bad."

A moment later, as she was checking my paperwork, she added, "I'm working sixteen hours today."

"Sixteen hours! How come?" I asked.

"Since they don't have a guardhouse," she explained, "they can't keep anybody. I don't mind. They always ask me. I always say yes." She paused a moment and added, "I get overtime pay practically every week."

I thought, "She has a racket going here!" As she handed my paperwork to me, I felt my air conditioning rushing out of my window into the broiling Texas heat. I offered, "I guess you'll be glad when they get a guardhouse built."

Her beautiful smile kicked up a few degrees and she leaned forward; in fact, she leaned so far forward she stuck her head in my window. She said, "Mister, I hope they never build one." And then instantly her smile disappeared, signaling she meant business when she said, "And when you fill out your customer evaluation, don't you recommend they build one, either."

She had an attitude of gratitude. She took a situation that most people would find intolerable, but instead of grumbling or quitting, she turned a lemon of a job into lemonade. That's an attitude of gratitude.

When you say "Thank you" forty times a day, it cultivates your optimistic perspective. You complain less and channel your energy into making things work, which is ultimately more satisfying. I recently read a story about a woman who, after sixteen years of being home raising her kids, went on job interviews. Potential employers were less than enthusiastic about her and kept her waiting. At first she was frustrated, wasting so many hours waiting, but during that time she realized other people also got frustrated waiting and that some were willing to pay so they didn't have to wait. Inspired by that thought, she started a waiting business. Now she sends her employees out to wait in people's homes for the gas company, furniture deliveries, cable TV installers, and others who are less than punctual. Her employees are housewives, too.

To my way of thinking, a person is not a success unless he is happy. And happy people are successful people. They have a thankful attitude. There is much to be thankful for and to be happy about right now. Choose to enjoy life and reflect that by finding at least forty things a day to feel thankful for.

Try 50 new things every month. Doesn't that sound obnoxious? Put it in perspective: that's fewer than two a day. And keep them simple. For example, here is something my wife, two kids, and I do every single time one of us goes to the grocery: We buy one item we have never bought before. It's fun, adventuresome, and it introduces us to new things we might have missed out on. Here are some other ideas: Go to work by a different route if you can, and let your brain cells get fired up playing with different visuals. Look up to the tops of buildings and trees; most Americans do not look any higher than their eyebrows. Add some adventure to lunch and choose something to eat that you have never had before. Stretch your creativity by writing your "to do" list in green ink and marking off completions in purple. Embrace the unexpected by browsing in the little hole-in-the-wall stores you never go into. Change your perspective on what life is all about by volunteering your next four Saturdays to work in a homeless shelter (and take your children with you).

Why bother? Doing fifty new things a month will help you get and stay comfortable with the rhythm of change. We are living in hyper-changing times and those who not only survive but also thrive are the ones who have gotten comfortable (not defensive) living with change. To make this your smartest year yet, let go of some comfortable habits because they hold you back. For example, instead of reading the newspaper first thing in the morning, grab a "how to" book in your hobby interest and read for ten minutes. Instead of waiting until you are in the mood to start a major project, tell yourself that you will block out thirty minutes today to get a portion of it going. Instead of leaving your job at the end of the day with a disheartening feeling of "Enough! I'll just deal with this stuff again tomorrow," use your last fifteen minutes to plan and prioritize your next day. Instead of leaving the game early so you can beat the traffic, stay and enjoy every moment and then have fun observing the world around you — so it takes an extra twenty minutes to get home. So what? Refuse to waste your energy on feeling aggravated.

Here's another reason to embrace change in a personal and continual way. Even if you were not in a confirmed journey to find greater success in your life, you would have to make big changes anyhow. Why? The Information Age is upon us.

At the start of the 21st century, the Information Age is actually a sweeping, world-wide revolution that is shaking up people's careers, as evidenced by how our jobs keep changing. Around us, we see corporate mergers, downsizing, restructuring, government and even military functions that are now out-sourced to private industry, and new growth industries that explode into our lives like rambunctious adolescent volcanoes. Your work has probably changed significantly. Many people tell me the jobs they are doing did not exist five years ago. Others laugh and say their jobs have evolved so much in just the last few months that they are nothing like the work they initially got hired to do.

To put these changes in perspective, consider this. The last big worldwide movement was the Industrial Age. It lasted approximately two hundred years. We are at the start of the Information Age. There is nothing on the horizon to foretell its slowing down, much less its end. Likely, we will live the remainder of our lives at the start of the Information Age. But you and I have people around us who think they are going to wait this thing out! They hunker down to keep things as they are. They are choosing not to participate in the changes. Say a prayer for them because they are as doomed as dinosaurs. The world is moving at an accelerating clip and has waning patience for people who choose not to keep up. The ones who will survive and thrive in our new environment are the ones who embrace change in a personal way. One method is to try fifty new things a month so that you are personally comfortable with the rhythm of change.

Do not forget to keep your relationships fresh, either. While speaking at a management retreat in Brattleboro, Vermont, I instructed the executive audience in the value of using this 10-20-30-40-50 Resiliency System to be the leaders that others would want to follow. At the conclusion, a young man came up to me and said, "Thank you!"

His energy was contagious so I beamed and said, "You're welcome! Thanks for what?"

"You just gave me my wife's birthday present," he exclaimed, "and I'm so excited right now I can't stand it!"

"Birthday present? What do you mean?" I asked.

"Tomorrow is her birthday," he explained. "We have been married for four years. We don't have a lot of money and I love her so much. I wanted this to be a special birthday. I didn't know what I was going to do, until you said, 'Try fifty new things a month.' That gave me an idea. Tomorrow, when she opens her card, I'm going to have written in it, 'I love you so much that every day for the next thirty days I'm going to dream up a fresh new way to tell you how much I love you.'"

Ahhhh. Isn't that romantic? What a nice guy. I suspect that most of the readers of this book would rather get a birthday gift like that than something off the shelf.

Let me ask you. Do you have somebody in your life you love more than anything in the world? What are you doing about it? You know, we could stop cars on the street and ask people how they show their love. Everyone would have a trunkload of intentions. That makes the market value for intentions exactly zero. What are you doing about it? I commend to you, for the next thirty days, dream up one fresh new way every day to say, "I love you." Watch what happens to the quality of the relationship. What happens to the quality of your RF. Best of all, watch what happens to the quality of your life! Denis Waitley says we become the people around us. But guess who the people around you are busy becoming? You! Be someone worth becoming. How to do that? There are lots of ways to become stronger, better, high-energy people. One method is this 10-20-30-40-50 Resiliency System.

To keep your supply of RF abundant, make two copies of the following formula. Tape one onto your mirror at home and the other to the side of your monitor at work.

As my friend Mike says, "If you don't ask, you don't get." As you reach for the stars, one question to ask yourself, "Do I have enough rocket fuel?" You know the answer is yes if you use the tools for generating your supply. Let this 10-20-30-40-50 Resiliency System serve as a renewable resource for your personal energy. Have fun on your journey. And to make your trip even more satisfying, be sure to take other people to the stars with you!

10-20-30-40-50 Resiliency System

- For 10 minutes each morning, I'll read something inspirational, motivational, or instructional to raise my energy and launch my day with an optimistic perspective.
- I'll spend 20 minutes a day around positive, upbeat, optimistic people. I delight in their electricity, and I become the people around me.
- I'll say 30 positive things about myself to myself daily to affirm the best in me. I become what I think about.
- I'll say "thank you" 40 times a day. I choose to enjoy life with an attitude of gratitude. Life is good — right now!
- I'll try at least 50 new things a month — which is less than two a day! Embracing change daily builds my career, dissolves anxiety, and increases fun!

ABOUT
DOUG SMART, CSP

*C*all on Doug Smart to get participants laughing, learning and leading. *Doug works with leaders and teams who want to smooth the bumps of rapid change. His radio show for high achieving business people, Smarter by the Minute, is broadcast five days a week. He is a successful business owner and a former top salesperson who is authoritative and authentic. Doug has spoken at over 1,000 conventions, conferences, seminars, sales rallies and management retreats.*

Doug is the author or co-author of Where There's Change There's Opportunity!, TimeSmart: How Real People Really Get Things Done at Work, TimeSmart: How Real People Really Get Things Done at Home, Reach for the Stars, Sizzling Customer Service, Brothers Together *and* FUNdamentals of Outstanding Teams. *The National Speakers Association awarded him the prestigious Certified Speaking Professional designation, an honor held by less than nine percent of the 4,000 members. Call or e-mail Doug's office for an information kit on bringing The Get Smart Series to your organization.*

Contact Information:
Doug Smart, CSP
Doug Smart Seminars
P.O. Box 768024
Roswell, GA 30076
Phone: (770) 587-9784
Fax: (770) 587-1050
E-mail: Doug@DougSmart.com
Website: www.DougSmart.com

SUCCESS IS AN ATTITUDE!
HOW TO GET WHAT YOU WANT
BY CHOOSING TO BE HAPPY

by Pamela Jett Aal, M.S.

Sisyphus of Greek mythological fame offended the gods. So, he was condemned to spend eternity rolling a rock up a hill, only to have it roll down again. He had to run down after it and begin to push the rock up the hill again. Forever. Over and over and over again. All his effort and energy amounted to nothing. Do you ever feel like Sisyphus? Stuck in a rut, doing the same things over and over and over again and not finding a reward or payoff? Do you find yourself exhausted at the end of the day, but not exactly sure what you have accomplished? Do you see people in your professional career who seem to be happy, infused with inner joy and spark, and wish that could be you? But you have no idea how to go about it? So you continue to roll your rock, day in and day out.

Finding the joy, direction, and success you have been yearning for is not easy, but it is simple. In fact, it can happen by integrating eight simple success principles and seven action steps into your life on a regular basis. They have all been road tested, and they have a proven track record of success. None are complex. In fact, they are very simple. There is, of course, a profound difference between simple and easy. They require us to step out of our comfort zone and do some things differently. I often advise attendees in my training sessions that if they are 100 percent happy with the results in their lives, both personally and professionally, not to change a thing. However, most of us want improvement in our relationships, careers, and our lives. What awaits you in the rest of this chapter is not feel-good fluff, not theory. What awaits you are solid principles and doable action steps to increase your joy, productivity, and to help you enjoy wholehearted success.

So, if you are tired of sharing Sisyphus's fate, the process can begin now. In this *very* moment as you sit reading *this* chapter in *this* very book.

Start in *this* instant to practice the first principle: **choose to be happy**. Wherever you are, whatever you have just experienced, whatever awaits you, make at this very moment a conscious choice to be happy.

In the course of some extraordinary research, Rick Foster and Greg Hicks discovered something fascinating.[1] They went into organizations and asked people like you "who is the happiest person you know?" After awhile, a pattern emerged. The same people were named over and over again. So the researchers went to those individuals and posed this simple question: how do you do it? Your friends and colleagues all say you are one of the happiest people they know. What is your secret?

The consistency of answers was amazing. These people did not lead charmed lives. In fact, many of these very happy people had faced tremendous challenges, difficulty, and even tragedy. Yet, they were still happy. So how did they answer? Quite simply. They said they were happy because they chose to be happy.

These individuals intimately understand the value of choosing your attitude. They know that if you get up in the morning and tell yourself before your feet hit the floor, "Ugh, it's going to be a bad day today," you have guaranteed yourself a bad day. It becomes a self-fulfilling prophecy. These very happy people understand that if it works to tell yourself you are having a bad day, it also works to tell yourself you are having a good day.

Most of us are wise enough not to get up the morning and tell ourselves, " I choose misery." The problem is, most of us stay neutral. We don't tell ourselves anything. Then we let circumstances, events, other people, and things like a traffic jam or a crabby boss take charge of our attitude and our day.

Happy people do have challenges. However, they are able to deal with them more effectively because of the optimistic attitude they begin each day with. It is true. Our attitude does determine our altitude.

If all this sounds a bit over the top or too good to be true, remember these are the techniques very happy people use. They have a proven record of success. Plus, there is no risk. No one needs to know you are doing it. While many behavioral psychologists will emphasize the importance of using affirmations and saying them aloud, I have also found by simply waking up every morning and placing the "I choose to be happy" thought in my head, I am leading a healthier, happier, more productive life. I remind myself, even in challenging situations, that while I may not have control over events, I do have control over my attitude — how I choose to view and respond to events.

There are some days when I need to remind myself to choose to be happy over and over and over again. However, even in the midst of having one of *those* days, by choosing to be happy, we can learn to train ourselves to be an optimist, not a pessimist. We can decide, every day, what kind of day we will have.

Action Step 1: Choose to be happy!
Right now, in this moment, no matter what!

For some of us, practicing this action step will be easier than for others. That is because of what researchers call our happiness set point.[2] Some people are inherently happier than others due to genetics and upbringing. However, regardless of our happiness set point, we can always choose to be happier. We can become more optimistic and less pessimistic. We, and only we, have control over our outlook and attitude.

Once we choose to be happy, we can move on to success principle two: **avoid toxic people**. Toxic people are those walking black holes of misery who seem to have one goal in life — sucking everyone else down with them. Remember, attitudes are contagious and theirs is not worth catching! There is a difference, of course, between a good friend who is having a difficult day and needs a shoulder to lean on and a toxic person. Toxic people are constantly finding the negative. They always have something critical or negative to say. And no matter what, they are miserable.

Some of you might be reading this thinking, "Pamela, I *can't* avoid toxic people! I gave birth to one, I'm married to one, I work with one — they are everywhere!" Notice, the advice is not to purge toxic people from your life, but to avoid them. When you have a choice, choose to be with the optimists, not the pessimists. Associate yourself with positive people, people who build you up, not tear you down. Be with the winners, not the whiners!

For example, if you have been invited out to lunch by the gossips, whiners and complainers, or you can eat your lunch by yourself out of a brown bag and it is an old turkey sandwich, which ought you to choose? The turkey sandwich, by yourself, of course!

Some of you might be thinking, "But Pamela, I can cheer them up!" As nice and altruistic as that sounds, it normally doesn't work. Toxic people, by and large, have chosen their attitude (toxic) and are comfortable there. What happens when we try to cheer up toxic people is we spend too much of our time and effort and energy for little to no payoff. I encourage you to think of someone who is toxic and then ask yourself, "How promotable are they?" The answer, of course, is — not very. Remember also the old adage — guilty by association. Even if you can cheer up a toxic person, it is high risk. You don't want to run the risk that someone else would think that you are toxic because of whom you associate with.

Action Step 2: Avoid Toxic People!

You may be thinking to yourself that all this sounds good; you will choose to be happy and avoid toxic people. However, you are not convinced that I know what it is like where you work. You find that since you work in a cube farm, like many of us do, that the miserable, toxic people come trudging up to you every day with their bad attitude showing and saying something like, "Is it Friday yet?" in that moan and groan tone.

Would you like to know what to do with *them* — the toxic people you try to avoid, but who don't get the hint and still come after you? When I ask this question in workshops, people always get a desperate look on their faces and almost beg for the answer. The secret to dealing with toxic people who come trudging up to you lies in the third success principle: **train other people how to treat you**.

Of course, for this to work we have to realize that we can't make toxic people not be toxic. But we can train them that their toxic attitude doesn't work with us: that while other people may get sucked into their misery, we don't function that way.

So, when the toxic person approaches you, I advise you to smile a little bit and respond that you are having a good day today or some other positive notion. I guarantee you, you will annoy the toxic person with your positive outlook and he or she will go away.

Will the person go away for good? No, of course not. The toxic person will wonder what you had in your cereal that morning that made you so perky and the next day will be right back at you with more negativity. So, smile, say something positive, and eventually he or she will figure something out: that you are no fun and someone else will make a better victim.

Bear in mind the management principle of "what gets rewarded gets repeated." If you constantly find miserable, toxic people coming to you, it may be time to ask yourself a tough question, "What am I doing that makes it so rewarding for them to be here?" For most of us the answer is listening, commiserating, participating.

I am not suggesting that you be mean, rude and nasty to toxic people. Simply stop giving them what they are looking for, and they will figure out that, while they may be toxic with other people, it does not work with you. Remember that you cannot make toxic people not be toxic. But you can train them how to treat you, and they will take their toxicity elsewhere.

Action Step 3:
Stop Rewarding Toxic People and Toxic Behavior

Now that we have three action steps in place we can work the fourth success principle: Practice **positive self-talk**. Research suggests that people talk to themselves at a rate of 600 to 800 words per minute. And, we believe the things we say when we talk to ourselves because we have no motivation to lie. Behavioral psychologists suggest that approximately three-fourths of what we say when we talk to ourselves is negative. We say things such as "I can't"; "I always mess this up"; "why bother, nobody cares what I think anyway"; or "I'm *just* a _____." The list could go on and on and on! And what is even more tragic is that sometimes the things we say to ourselves actually come flying out of our mouths! How can we expect other people to recognize our strengths when all we do is highlight our weaknesses?

Successful people recognize the power of self-talk and they chose to be their biggest fans, not their most vocal critics. The scary thing is most of us are unaware of how negative we are. And we are unaware of how our negative thinking impacts our success. There is profound truth in the adage that whether we think we can or can't, we're right.

If you are looking for a great way to discover if you are your own biggest fan or biggest critic, I challenge you to practice the following action step.

Action Step 4: Accept *All* Compliments with a "Thank You!"

Most of us brush off compliments. We have yet to learn to graciously accept them. And when we fail to accept them, not only are we being rude, but we are also denying ourselves vital emotional nutrition. Once you put this action step into practice, you will become much more aware of your own negativity. And, once you are aware, you can replace the negative with the positive. Which leads us to our fifth success principle: **practice optimistic criticism.**

Notice the wording: optimistic criticism, not constructive criticism. Constructive implies a building up while criticism implies breaking down to find fault. We cannot simultaneously build up and break down. Constructive criticism is an oxymoron.

There is nothing wrong with recognizing our faults, weaknesses, and mistakes. But, how we talk to ourselves about them is vitally important. When successful people make a mistake, they follow the advice of General George Patton who once said, "The only failure is when we fail to learn from our mistakes."

If a successful person makes a mistake at work which of the following do you think is more likely to be the response, scenario A or scenario B?

Scenario A

A mistake is made at work, a fairly costly one. Person A, driving home from work, mutters phrases such as, "I can't believe I did that," "I am soooo stupid," "It will be a miracle if this doesn't come up during my annual review." "I don't know what I was thinking; I should never have taken such a risk!"

or

Scenario B

A mistake is made at work, a fairly costly one. Person B drives home from work thinking, "I made a mistake today." "Next time, what will I do differently?" "Is there anything I like about what I did?" "What did I learn from this experience?"

The answer is obvious; the successful person would use the language of scenario B, acknowledging the mistake (criticism) and learning from it, and then focusing on the future (optimism).

What is even more interesting is to project our scenarios out to the next day. Which person would bring more value back to the workplace the next day? The person being merely critical, or the person practicing optimistic criticism? Again, the answer is obvious!

Action Step 5:
Integrate "Next time, I will . . ." into your self-talk

Successful people know they cannot change the past; they can only fix the future. So, when they talk to themselves, they stay focused on future solutions, not past problems. Instead of beating themselves up when they make a mistake, they focus on how to respond the next time.

Successful people are clearly future focused. They don't dwell on the past or the "what ifs" of life or the "if onlys." They focus on what comes next. They practice success principle six: **visualize success**.

Many of us spend a tremendous amount of time rolling our rocks up mountains because we think it is what we are supposed to do in order to make everybody else happy. We wind up feeling exhausted and without a sense of accomplishment. Successful people understand that success comes from an internal locus of control as opposed to an external locus of control. They understand that since no one can make us happy unless we choose to be happy, then we cannot make other people happy.

Successful individuals know what success means to them. Not what other people feel ought to be a measuring stick for success, but what they feel is the measuring stick. For some successful people, success means financial stability coupled with a stable marriage and a rich family life. For others success means they have achieved fame and fortune in their industry. For yet others, it is putting in an honest day's work for an honest day's pay with time to pursue leisure activities, hobbies, and community service. It doesn't matter to them if others do not think they are successful. They measure success by their own personal standards.

To see if you are currently living this principle, I challenge you at this very moment to finish the following sentence:

Success = _____

Successful people can not only finish that sentence; they can describe success in vivid, rich detail. Consider the story of Laura Wilkinson, the 2000 Olympic Gold Medallist in the women's 10-meter platform dive. Six months before the Olympics, she could not walk, let alone dive, due to a broken foot. To keep training as she healed, she dove every day in her mind. She went through every moment and imagined a perfect dive in vivid detail, every time. Still wearing a foot brace to assist her as she climbed the platform, she went on to an upset gold medal victory over the favored Chinese divers. Part of the secret to her success was that she consistently imagined it in vivid, accurate detail.

Successful people can give you that same vivid detail if you ask them what they will be doing in 5, 10, 15 years. And the amazing thing is, research proves they are more likely to achieve that vision.

Action Step 6: Finish the sentence "success = _____ to me."

But of course, a vision without a plan is just a wish. Successful people practice success principle seven: they are **goal setters**. They set both short and long-term goals to assist them in reaching their vision of success. They write their goals down in the present tense such as " in the fourth quarter I have a 10 percent increase in sales" or "I read to my child four nights a week for at least a half hour." They recognize that what gets measured gets done, so they make their goals measurable. Additionally, successful people review their goals regularly and monitor their progress. A simple way to review your goals regularly is to employ the following:

Action Step 7: Post your success vision and goals where you can see them regularly.

Many people choose to put their success vision on the ceiling of their bedroom so it is the first thing they see in the morning, or on the bathroom mirror, or make it their computer screen saver. Successful people do this because it is very difficult to work on the wrong thing when the right thing is right in front of you.

Obviously, the path of successful people towards their goals is not unimpeded. Yet, they consistently practice success principle eight: **move personal mountains**. The philosopher Keirkegaard tells a story of a man who went on a long journey. In the middle of his journey he came to a huge mountain. Instead of going around the mountain, going over the mountain, or even tunneling through the mountain, he sat and waited for the mountain to move. He waited for God or some other higher power to move that obstacle out of his way. He eventually grew old and died sitting at the foot of the mountain waiting for the mountain to move. I challenge you to ask yourself "what is my mountain?" What is standing in the way of my success that I am failing to take action on? What am I waiting for someone else to take care of for me?

For some of us it is fear; for some of us it is self-discipline; for others it is lack of skills, self-confidence or energy. Sometimes the mountain will be big, sometimes small. A common mountain is the mountain of excuse: "I'll do it later," "I don't have time," "It's too expensive." Regardless of your mountain, I challenge you, whatever it is that is standing in the way of your vision of success, do something, do anything about it! Take action! Not tomorrow, but today. Don't wait for someone else to take care of it for you. Successful people are proactive, nor reactive. They don't wait for others to take care of what they could be taking care of for themselves.

There is an old saying that *knowledge absorbed is knowledge. Knowledge applied is wisdom.*

Apply the knowledge of the success principles. Take the challenge of the action steps. Start in this very instant to choose to be happy no matter what, and you are well on your way to being a winner, not a whiner. Well on your way to avoiding the fate of Sisyphus and finding the joy, direction and the wholehearted success you have been yearning for.

Action Step Reminder

1. I can choose to be happy! Right now, in this moment, no matter what!
2. I can avoid toxic people.
3. I can stop rewarding toxic people and toxic behavior.
4. I can accept all compliments with a thank you.
5. I can integrate "next time I will" into my self-talk.
6. I can finish the sentence "success = _____ to me."
7. I can post my success vision and goals where I can see them regularly.

[1]Rick Foster and Greg Hicks, *How We Choose to Be Happy: The 9 Choices of Extremely Happy People — Their Secrets, Their Stories*, G. P. Putnam's Sons, New York, New York, 1999.

[2]Dr. David Lykken, Happiness: *The Nature and Nurture of Joy and Contentment*, St. Martin's Griffin, New York, New York, 1999.

ABOUT
PAMELA JETT AAL, M.S.

*P*amela Jett Aal is President of Jett Communication Training, Inc., an organization committed to helping groups, businesses and individuals increase productivity, profits and performance by decreasing miscommunication, stress, and conflict. With over a decade of experience, Pamela brings a high-energy, how-to approach to every keynote presentation or training session. A motivating keynote speaker and a skilled trainer in areas such as stress management, dealing with difficult people, customer service, time management and interpersonal communication skills, Pamela delivers solutions.

Her audiences rave about her sense of humor, emphasis on practical application and solutions to challenging issues. Satisfied clients include Compaq Computers, Wal-Mart, Lockheed Martin, Hitachi Semiconductors, The United Way, and the U.S. Air Force. Pamela works with individuals and organizations, both large and small, in the U.S. and around the world.

Contact Information:
Pamela Jett Aal, M.S.
Jett Communication Training, Inc.
P.O. Box 10745
Bakersfield, CA 93389
Phone: (661) 637-1922
E-mail: Pamela@JettCT.com
Website:www.JettCT.com

NOTES

NOTES

Resource Listing

Pamela Jett Aal, M.S.
Jett Communication Training, Inc.
P.O. Box 10745
Bakersfield, CA 93389
Phone: (661) 637-1922
E-mail: Pamela@JettCT.com
Website: www.JettCT.com

Sharon Baker
Let's Talk . . . RESULTS, inc.
2790 Paso Del Norte Drive Suite #1
Indianapolis, IN 46227
Phone: (317) 859-1214
Fax: (317) 859-1215
E-mail: queene412@aol.com

Pauline George, M.Ed.
PG Training & Consulting
1104 Forest Edge Court
Wexford, PA 15090
Phone: (724) 934-2836
Fax: (724) 934-2838
E-mail: PGtrain@attglobal.net
Website: www.PGtrain.com

Cecilia B. Grimes
Etiquette Matters
513 West Glendale Street
Siler City, NC 27344
Phone: (919) 742-3616
E-mail:
    EtiquetteMatters@mindspring.com
Website: www.EtiquetteMatters.com

Tom Guzzardo
Guzzardo Leadership Group
109 Holly Ridge Road
Stockbridge, GA 30281
Phone: (770) 474-1889
Fax: (770) 474-0442
E-mail: Guzzardo22@aol.com
Website: www.TomGuzzardo.com

D.J. Harrington, CSP
Phone Logic, Inc.
2820 Andover Way
Woodstock, GA 30189
Phone: (770) 516-7796
Fax: (770) 516-7797
E-mail: DJHarrington@mindspring.com
Website: www.DJHarrington.com

Max Howard
Max Howard Associates
429 Rays Road
Stone Mountain, GA 30083
Phone: (404) 296-8963
Fax: (404) 294-0670
E-mail: Max@MaxSpeaks.com
Website:www.MaxSpeaks.com.

James W. Hunt
eChange2, Inc.
P.O. Box 2726
Alpharetta, GA 30023-2726
Phone: (770) 751-8763
E-mail: JWHunt@eChange2.com>
Website: www.eChange2.com

Charlene Lockwood, M.A.
NMX Inc.
P.O. Box 66805
Phoenix, AZ 85082
Phone: (602) 524-4354
Pager: (888) 506-4499
E-mail: CKLockwood@msn.com

Natalie Manor
Natalie Manor Associates
P.O. Box 1508
Merrimack, NH 03054
Phone: (800) 666-2230
Fax: (603) 424-1267
E-mail:
  CoachNatalie@ManorEvents.mv.com
Website:
  www.NatalieManorAssociates.com

Chet R. Marshall
130 Summit Ridge
Hurricane, WV 25526
Phone: (304) 757-1985
E-mail: ChetinWV@aol.com

Snowden McFall
Fired Up!
74 Northeastern Blvd., Unit 20
Nashua, NH 03062
Phone: (603) 882-0600
Fax: (603) 882-5979
E-mail:
  SMcFall@FiredUp-TakeAction-Now.com
Websites:
  www.FiredUp-TakeAction-Now.com
  www.BrightworkAdvertising.com

Betty Pichon
6821 E. Thunderbird Road
Scottsdale, AZ 85254
Phone: (480) 596-7997
Fax: (480) 596-5237
E-mail: BPichon956@aol.com

Michael E. Rega
Ecliptic Consulting Group, Inc./
Persuasive Communication
P.O. Box 23807
Tempe, AZ 85285
Phone (800) 236-2980
Fax: (480) 899-3015
E-mail: AZEcliptic@aol.com
Website: www.ecgpc.com